The
Cape Herders

A History of the Khoikhoi of Southern Africa

The
Cape Herders

A History of the Khoikhoi of Southern Africa

Emile Boonzaier
Candy Malherbe
Andy Smith
and
Penny Berens

DAVID PHILIP
Cape Town & Johannesburg

OHIO UNIVERSITY PRESS
Athens

2nd impression 2000

First published 1996 in southern Africa by
David Philip Publishers (Pty) Ltd,
208 Werdmuller Centre, Claremont, 7700, South Africa

& in the United States of America by
Ohio University Press, Scott Quadrangle, Athens
Ohio, 45701

ISBN 0 86486 311 X (David Philip)
ISBN 0 8214 1174 8 (Ohio University Press)

© 1996 Emile Boonzaier, Candy Malherbe,
Andy Smith and Penny Berens

Library of Congress Cataloging-in-Publication data
available

Printed by Clyson Printers
11th Avenue, Maitland, Cape Town

Contents

List of Illustrations

Introduction

The main attraction of the Cape in the early days of trade between Europe and the East Indies was the availability of cattle, the domestic stock of the indigenous herders. This book looks at the history and way of life of these people and tries to show how important they have always been in the development of South African society.

The name 'Hottentot' was a collective name given to the people of the Cape by early travellers from Europe. There are several possible origins for this name. In 1616, the English traveller Edward Terry said they were called this because of their click language, which resembled the 'clucking of hens, or the gobbling of turkeys'. In 1620 a French commander reported, among many other things, that the 'usual greeting' of the Cape people was 'to dance a song, of which the beginning, the middle and the end is *hautitou*'; a little later, this expression was recorded by a Dane as 'Hottentott'. 'Hottentot' became used in Europe to refer to the indigenous people at the Cape of Good Hope. Whatever the reason, it was not a name they would have used for themselves. In fact, a collective name was probably not used, although some scholars have suggested that the name 'Khoikhoi' or 'Khoekhoe', meaning 'the real people' or 'real men', derived from *khoib* (a man) or *khoii* (a person), would have been acceptable. The names they would have used for themselves would have been their clan names, such as 'Cochoqua', 'Goringhaiqua', 'Gorachoqua', and so on. To simplify matters we are going to use the name 'Khoikhoi', as this is the word most often used in the literature.

The use of names

The Khoikhoi called themselves 'the real people' to distinguish themselves from other groups, such as the San (Soaqua or Sonqua), called Bushmen by the colonists, who were people living off the veld and who had no cattle. Therefore San was a term denoting lower status. In modern Nama orthography, the spelling of Khoikhoi would be *Khoekhoe*. Other variations on the name were *Kwena*, or *Khoe-na*. The word 'Khoisan' is used as a wider term for the racial stock to which both Khoikhoi and Bushmen belong (and for the click languages which they both speak) or for people who are difficult to distinguish, especially during the later colonial period when refugees were moving away from the Cape and mixing with other groups in the hinterland.

Over the centuries many myths have grown up about 'Hottentots'. One of these has been that they are people 'of inferior intellect or culture' (see 'Hottentot' in the *Universal Oxford Dictionary* as recently as 1955). In 1726 the 4th Earl of Chesterfield could refer to one of his rivals in these terms: 'The utmost I can do for him is to consider him a respectable Hottentot.' Thus even in the English language the name 'Hottentot' had a pejorative meaning. Why should this be the case? What was it that placed the herding people of the Cape in such low standing with those of Western Europe? We hope to be able to show that the force of such perceptions not only influenced the early European travellers, but had a negative effect on these original inhabitants.

Who were the Khoikhoi? How did they relate to the Bushmen? These are two questions which keep cropping up in the discussion of pre-colonial history of the Cape. Since academics do not always agree on the definitions, and human sciences grow from new data appearing all the time, it is not surprising that people get confused over the history of the Cape's aboriginal inhabitants. It is even more confusing when we try to place people within their correct time period, because categories and names change through time, depending on who is describing them and how they use their names. Even more confusion is created by mixing up language categories with cultural and bio-physical differences. As a result, people who do not know how to separate and evaluate the different bits of information build up, in their minds, a hodge-podge of stereotypes which has little to do with historical reality, as we understand it in the 1990s.

The purpose of this book is to try to separate the different categories and use them to produce a reasonably accurate picture of the past, and to look in particular at the development of herding society in southern Africa and how it was adapted to the western Cape.

The nomadic herders at the Cape were some of the first Africans practising this type of economy whom travellers from Europe met. They had already been established at the southern tip of the continent for over a thousand years when Bartolomeu Dias rounded the Cape and became the first European to meet the Khoikhoi (in 1488, at what is today Mossel Bay). Khoikhoi herders, seemingly in control of the winter rainfall area of the Cape, capitulated fairly swiftly to the early Dutch settlers at Table Bay. The story of their subjugation and eventual incorporation into colonial society is a theme of this book. We have tried to show how their incorporation as lower class menials in settler society was accomplished by force and by the removal of their means of livelihood. As we shall show this was accompanied by ideological forces which made the Khoikhoi accept their marginal position in society as being correct, even though their contribution to the colonial economy was crucial for its continued survival.

The view of the Khoikhoi has always been through European eyes. We have attempted to look at Khoikhoi history and social formations from both sides, using a combination of archaeology, history and social anthropology to build up a picture of how they used the land and how they modified land usage through time, under the pressure of new economic and social forces.

Figure 1. Khoikhoi family in the early 1700s. Artist unknown, SA Library.

3

Pre-colonial history of the Cape

1

The pre-colonial period is one for which there are no written records, and all information on the Khoikhoi has to come from a wide range of sources, most of which are archaeological. This period includes both the pre-colonial and the early period of contact with Europeans, before the lifestyle of the Khoikhoi was irreparably changed by European settlement at the Cape.

The raw data of archaeology are the material remains left by people. No one can avoid discarding things, whether they be the by-products of everyday life, such as food remains, or the unwanted parts people discard when making things, or even parts of people themselves, when they die. Alone, a single piece of stone, metal, pottery, bone, plastic or tin can tell us a little about the people who used it. But along with other discarded things we can build up a picture, if not of an individual, at least of the social group. The most basic things, such as garbage found in a household dustbin, can give us clues to what a family did since the bin was last emptied. If we had the accumulated rubbish of this family, discarded daily, for a whole year, we would probably be able to say quite a lot

Archaeological sites

A large part of archaeological fieldwork involves digging up things left behind when people go away. These things can inform us about the lifestyle of the past. In some places people stayed for a long time, or came back for repeated occupations, and so threw away a lot of rubbish. This means the sites can be found easily, and the large amount of rubbish increases the chances of at least some of it surviving into the present. A basic principle that archaeologists use is that the things which were thrown away first will be at the bottom of the garbage heap, and more recently discarded things will be found at the top. When archaeologists dig they keep a complete record of where artefacts (the things people made) came from at each level of the excavation. Since we know people in the past had fashions or styles which they preferred, by comparing each level with the one above we can see how the style of artefacts may have changed through time.

Ideally, archaeologists would like to see the remains in position exactly as they were used or dropped before the people left, since where each thing is in relation to the others will tell us more about what the people were doing than just the isolated pieces themselves. For example, on many archaeological sites in the south-western Cape we find large quantities of broken ostrich eggshell. Some of the pieces have been made into beads, but only on those sites where the broken fragments of bead-making have been thrown away can we say the beads were actually being made on the site. The position of the beads that are found on the site, such as around the fireplace, will tell us about how the area of the site was used.

This is why it is important not to pick up old pottery, stone, bone, glass or ostrich eggshells, but to tell the local museum or archaeology department if you find a site.

Unfortunately, not all things survive. Organic remains, such as skin or wood, tend to break down and disappear, so that only on sites found in special locations, where unusual conditions have prevailed, will the organic pieces survive. Such conditions are very arid environments (the desiccation of materials in ancient Egypt has meant many wooden and leather objects have been found by archaeologists), or waterlogging (skin and wood do not decay in peat bogs or in silts under the ocean). Some very dry caves in the western Cape have preserved pieces of leather, wood and fibres, so we know the pre-colonial people used string and leather bags.

Sometimes materials are disturbed after they are left. This happens in two ways: disturbance by natural agents, such as wind and water erosion; and disturbance by human action, such as digging foundations for buildings.

When disturbance has taken place archaeologists say that the material is no longer in 'primary context' (where it was left), but in 'secondary context' (where it ended up). If we want to learn about humans in the past, primary context material is the most useful.

about their lifestyle, seasonal preferences, and where they fitted into the society at large. This is why detectives following up clues usually collect all the litter they can find at the scene of a crime.

The great problem with the material remains left by people is that over time, organic things tend to disintegrate and disappear. This means that archaeological residues that are old are only a tiny fraction of an entire society's discards. It also means that it is all the more important that when an archaeologist excavates a site, a record is kept of exactly where the things were found in the ground. The position of the surviving pieces in relation to each other can tell something about those things which have disappeared through not being preserved.

An example of this can be seen from the archaeological site of Kasteelberg, near Saldanha Bay in the western Cape.

Dating archaeological remains

There are two main ways in which we know how old things are on archaeological sites:

Relative dating. The oldest things are normally found at the bottom of a site, and younger things further up in the excavation. By knowing where things came from in the site we can learn that a certain style of object may differ from another. Thus the age of one artefact can be said to be older than the other. By excavating many sites we can build up a 'relative' sequence to compare the ages of the different occupations by people across a large site, a valley or even a region; but there is no way of knowing how many years ago the site was occupied.

Absolute dating. Here we can give an age in years, such as 2,300 BP (before the present). The simplest absolute dating is to tie an excavation into a calendar which we can match with our own present-day calendar system. An example of this would be knowing how the Mayans of Mexico counted their years and organised their calendar.

Another technique is radiocarbon dating. This is a method which requires a sophisticated chemical laboratory. It is based on the fact that there are several isotopes of carbon, one of which, carbon 14, is radioactive. In other words, it decays at a predictable rate and gives off energy through time. In the atmosphere, normal carbon is composed of both stable and unstable (or radioactive) isotopes. When an animal or plant is alive it absorbs both of these isotopes. Once the organism dies, it stops absorbing carbon, and the radioactive isotope begins to decay. Thus the proportion of stable to unstable carbon isotopes will change the longer the animal or plant has been dead. Being able to measure the ratio of the one against the other can indicate the time since the animal or plant died. Giving the actual year of the animal's or plant's death requires knowing the rate at which carbon 14 disappears. Scientists have worked out that every 5 568 years half of the radioactive material is lost, and so they can give a number of radiocarbon years since the animal or plant died. Some of the best material for dating by this method is charcoal, and since people lived around fires, this is often found on sites.

This site was occupied by herding people who were probably the ancestors of the Khoikhoi. We found a tiny lamb skeleton whose bones were complete, covered in red pigment. None of the bones surrounding the skeleton, however, had any red staining on them. This tells us that the whole lamb was covered in pigment when it was buried. The lamb must have been wrapped in something, otherwise all the other bones around would have had pigment on them. The wrapping, possibly a skin, had disappeared by the time we did the excavation some 900 years later. Why would people coat a lamb in pigment and then bury it without eating it? We have to use other information for a possible answer. We know that herding people elsewhere in Africa sacrifice animals during religious occasions – to give thanks when their children are born, or as a sign of respect for their relatives when they die, just as Muslims do during Eid today, and as people did in biblical times. The little lamb from Kasteelberg is a small clue to the religious beliefs of the early herders of the Cape.

Figure 2. The three main pottery decoration types at the Kasteelberg site, showing the percentages in different levels through time. What can be seen is that the decoration virtually disappears about 1 000 BP (before the present), and only plain pots were made after this time. Knowing roughly the order in which decorations appeared allows archaeologists to build a sequence for relative dating.

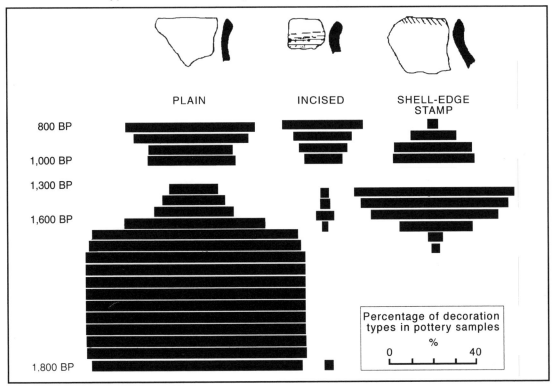

'Savages'.
Figure 3 (left). Lin-schoten (1599).
Figure 4 (below). Her-bert (1634).

Europeans and 'savages' at the Cape

In the Middle Ages, Africa was known to Europe only from vague accounts of a mythical king, Prester John, who lived beyond the edges of the 'Christian' world centred on the Mediterranean. Accounts of people to be found in Africa came from Greek and Roman sources, and they included descriptions of monstrous people who had names like Blemmyae (people with faces on their chests), Scopapods (one-legged people), Troglodytae (blind people living in caves) and Garamantes (sexually promiscuous people) among others. Another group were Anthropophages (man-eaters), who could be recognised by their ugliness.

The first travellers to the 'edges' of the world thus expected to meet these monstrous races. What they found, of course, were other humans, but so different from themselves that the Europeans had no difficulty placing them into one or other of the expected categories. This was especially true of the Khoikhoi, who were described by Augustin de Beaulieu in 1620 in the following way: 'The inhabitants of the country towards the point of the Cape are, I believe, the most miserable savages which have been discovered up to now, since they know nothing of sowing or of gear for plough-

8

ing or cultivating the soil.'

John Jourdain, in 1608, thought they might be cannibals: '… they could come to eat mans flesh, they would not make any scruple of it, for I think the world doth not yield a more heathenish people and more beastlie.'

The Khoikhoi therefore fitted into the category of Anthropophages, and a number of the earliest drawings of them highlight characteristics seen as 'beastly' and cannibalistic (figs 3 and 4). This image of the Khoikhoi was thus created by Europeans, and in some ways it has lasted to the present day.

With the foundation of the colony at Table Bay, day-to-day contact modified the impressions of the Europeans to a certain degree, since they were now dealing with real people. However, the ideology of superiority, along with an economy based on the merchant wealth of one of the world's great maritime empires,

Figure 5. 'Quaint people in Africa', Sebastian Münster (1544).

made it impossible for them to accept the Khoikhoi as equals. The Khoikhoi's infinitely superior ability to deal with the African environment was not given any value, even though this knowledge enabled the early colonists to adapt to the landscape as they trekked beyond the settlement of Cape Town. The many Khoikhoi words that exist in Afrikaans show how significant their way of life

Figure 6. Reports of people eating human flesh, as food or for ritual purposes, are numerous. Anthropologists point out that these are almost always second-hand accounts. This drawing from 1592 carries the idea of cannibalism to an absurd extreme.

'Cannibals'

Anthropologists point out that most reports of people eating human flesh, as food or for ritual purposes, are second-hand accounts, usually by people trying to damage the reputation of their enemies. In Europe in the 1600s 'cannibal' had the fascination of a freshly coined name for a shameful practice. It comes from the Spanish version of 'Carib', those West Indians who fiercely resisted the Conquistadores and gave their name to a string of islands and surrounding sea, the Caribbean. There is no evidence that the Khoikhoi were eaters of human flesh. However, in 1595 a voyager found reasons for supposing that they were: '… it looked as if they would have eaten some of us, since they made little ado of eating raw guts' (fig. 5). The English ship's pilot, John Davys, reported in 1598 that he and others who landed at the Cape 'stayed by our Tents, being belegred with Canibals and Cowes'.

When Europeans met hostility among the natives of the places where they called, they often referred to them as cannibals, a name which expressed their fears of the unknown, and which was used to justify, as self-defence, any steps they took against the native inhabitants.

was to the early colonists expanding into the interior.

Other names which keep cropping up in this early history of the Cape are 'strandlopers', and the names of Khoikhoi groups or clans. The word 'strandloper', or beach-ranger, comes from the observation by early settlers at the Cape of people living along the beach and subsisting on marine foods, such as seals, shellfish, fish, crayfish, birds and occasionally beached whales. The word could have been used either for hunters or herders, and merely refers to the exploitation of coastal resources.

Work done by Judy Sealy at the University of Cape Town in analysing the stable carbon isotope ratios of human skeletons to determine what people ate, has shown that some pre-colonial groups could have spent most of the year at the coast eating food from the sea.

Figure 7. Attitudes persist. This 1994 pre-election graffito has a message for coloured people. It suggests that if they vote for the National Party – architects of apartheid – they will remain 'Hottentots', in this case used as a word to describe people who are subservient and inferior.

Khoikhoi words and names in everyday use

There are many Khoikhoi words common in everyday Afrikaans and English speech in South Africa. There are the geographical place names such as Outeniqua, Karoo, Gamka, Namaqualand, Kamdeboo, Keiskamma and Troe-Troe. There are animal names – *gogga* (insect), *koedoe* (antelope), *kwagga* (zebra), *geitjie* (gecko) – and plant names – *boegoe* (*Agathosma* spp.), *dagga* (*Cannabis sativa*), *koekemakranka* (*Gethyllis* spp.), *kambro* (*Stapelia* spp.), *karree* (*Rhus* spp.) – and the names of things such as *karos* (cloak) and *kierie* (stick). The words refer to not just things and places, but also include *abba* (piggy-back), *kamma* (make-believe), *eina* (ouch) and *aitsa* (well-I-never).

Where did the Khoikhoi come from?

2
Interest in the origins of the herding people of South Africa has a long history. In the early period, sailors and other voyagers showed very little interest in these 'savages', other than using them as a means to obtain animals with which to provision their ships. Once the colony at the Cape was established in the 1600s the colonists began to be more aware of the Khoikhoi and started to refer to them by their own names, although few Dutch learned the Khoikhoi language.

By 1700, scientific enquiry into the order of things had awakened interest in the relationship between peoples. These enquiries led people to assume that the Khoikhoi were not native to southern Africa – a reasoning based on the biblical beliefs of the time. Kolb, in 1731, thought that the Khoikhoi were of Jewish origin: 'These Customs, in which the Hottentots agree with both the Jews and Troglodytes, being, 'tis pretty certain, all or most of 'em as old as the Time of Abraham, which was but 300 Years after the Flood, refer their Tradition so clearly to Noah, as to put the Matter almost out of Doubt.'

Fifty years later, Mentzel reiterated this theme, but with somewhat different conclusions:

One thing is indubitably certain that

both the tame and the wild Hottentots are descended together with all other human beings from common ancestors. Granting this, it is incredible and impossible to suppose that this nation could have come to the Southernmost point of Africa from Asia where without any doubt man first lived after the Deluge.

Mentzel goes on to discuss the barriers to migration between Asia and southern Africa and how little cultural similarity exists between the two areas. From this he could only deduce that the Khoikhoi were descended from children shipwrecked off the South African coast.

By 1800 it was generally recognised that the people of southern Africa were indeed African, and not Asian. However, all inhabitants of the southern end of the continent were supposed to have come from the north. After his travels during the years 1803–6, Hinrich Lichtenstein stated that 'the southern parts of Africa were originally peopled from the northern [parts]' with the 'Caffres remaining in the eastern parts ... but the Hottentots spreading towards the west, and even to the southern point.' Lichtenstein assumed a common source for both the 'Hottentots' and 'Caffres'. He went on to say:

on the flat, sandy plains along the Western coast ... the soil offers but poor resources for the support of life, which naturally leads the inhabitants of these parts rather to the hunter's than to the shepherd's life. The people then who wandered hither would consequently lose that degree of cultivation which was preserved among the inhabitants of the eastern coast, and from the instability of their lives, destitute of property,

would spread themselves continually, till reaching the southern extremity, they could go no further ... It was in this way that the Hottentots reached the Southern coast some centuries earlier than the Caffres. They were then in a situation to return somewhat to their pastoral life, and while the Gonacquas, situated on the fertile bank of the Chamtoo river, became peaceable and somewhat more civilised people than the Saabs ['Bushmen'], who remained on the dry and desert plains of the northern parts, sunk gradually to the very lowest step of physical and moral degradation ... At every step they made towards the east, the Hottentots found the country more fertile; they inhabited it therefore far beyond the present boundary between the colony and the Caffre country. For to this day many of the rivers and hills have Hottentot names ... But they were driven back by the Caffres, who in the meantime had come down from the north.

The idea of a northern 'homeland' of the Khoikhoi became generally accepted, and a century later, in 1905, George

Figure 8. Stow and Cooke models of Khoikhoi origins.

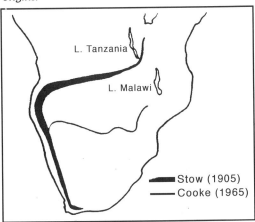

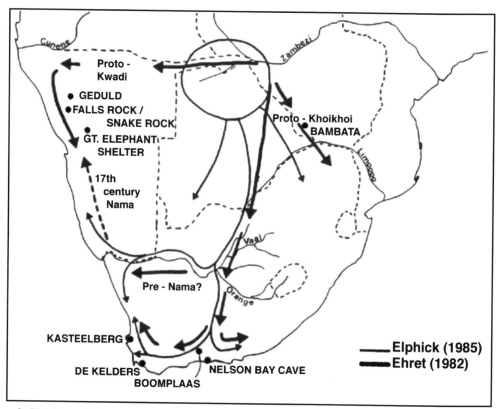

Figure 9. Elphick and Ehret models of Khoikhoi origins.

Stow described successive migrations from the north beginning with the Bushmen whose origin 'was far north of the equator'. He continued:

after the original Bushmen migration, the Hottentot tribes ... were the first to follow them. These people were themselves driven from the more central portions of the continent by another race still stronger than themselves. They then retreated in a south-westerly direction, until arrested by the Atlantic, when they turned towards the south. We shall find that in the meantime the tribes before whom the Hottentots fled were themselves pressed farther into Central Southern Africa, and away from the eastern coast, by still stronger and fiercer hordes from the north. The men who pressed forward the Hottentots were the Bachoana and Basutu hordes.

He referred directly to his idea of their point of origin when he discussed the 'yellow-skinned pastoral nomads ... from the intra-lacustrine regions of Central Africa' (fig. 8).

Today no serious scholar of African prehistory accepts an 'intra-lacustrine' source (between the East African lakes) for the Khoikhoi, although the 'Hamitic' (north-African) origin of the Khoikhoi is still to be found in some South African school texts, and at least one amateur historian is still convinced that the Khoikhoi language is derived from 'ancient Cretan and Anatolian languages'.

14

Domestic animals and Khoikhoi origins

The Khoikhoi were herders. To find out more about them we will have to look at the effects of the introduction of domestic animals into southern Africa.

Archaeological sites in the Sahara have produced the earliest dated bones of domestic animals in Africa. These date from about 7 000 years ago, and were found along with rock paintings in the mountains. Tsetse flies are fatal to domestic stock and these flies formed a barrier across the southern Sahara which prevented the southward spread of cattle and small stock until the Sahara dried up around 4 500 years ago. Archaeologists have been able to date domestic animals in east Africa to 4 000 years ago, where herding societies like the Maasai developed.

Just before the beginning of the Christian era, a new technology appeared in the central lakes district of east Africa: iron smelting. The people who developed this complicated technology were farmers and most likely came into contact with the herders already established there. As yet we do not know very much about the relationship between these farmers and the herders, but we do know that farmers obtained domestic stock, probably in return for grain from their fields. Elsewhere in the world there are records of nomadic herdsmen who put pressure on agricultural people, and who may even have exacted tribute from them at harvest time. Whatever the social relations and outside pressures, the farmers began to move southwards, so that by 100 BC they were in what is now Zambia and Zimbabwe with their herds and domestic crops. Their metal tools allowed them to clear the land efficiently for preparing their fields, and so they were able to move into densely

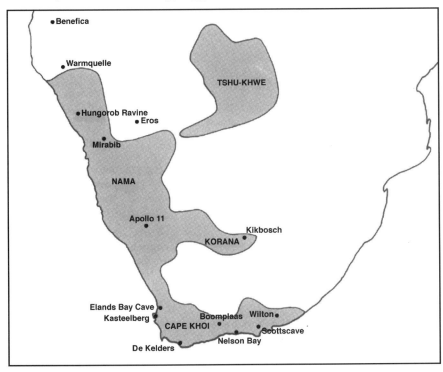

Figure 10. Experts who study languages believe that people who spoke the Khoikhoi language once lived in the areas shaded on the map. Archaeologists have found remains of livestock and pottery at the places named on this map.

15

Different ideas about the origins of herding societies of southern Africa

Not everyone agrees with the timing of the transfer of stock from an incoming African agro-pastoralist society to an aboriginal hunting society, creating Khoikhoi pastoralism.

The anthropologist Ed Wilmsen notes that 'much of the basic pastoral vocabulary used by speakers of southern Bantu languages is derived through a Khoisan intermediary'. This suggests that the Khoikhoi were in possession of domestic stock before these Bantu-speakers arrived in southern Africa. However, another theory, put forward by the historical linguist Ehret, notes that:

Whereas Khoikhoi words for 'ram', 'young ram' and 'ewe' can all be shown to be probable loan-words from a non-Khoikhoi language, for cattle only the generic term *komo- is an apparent loan. Although the earliest Khoikhoi therefore knew of cattle, it is for sheep that a clear breeding terminology is indicated. The Khoikhoi coinage of most of their specifically bovine breeding terms thus may well betoken a more gradual growth of acquaintance with cattle.

Certainly the earliest domestic animals showing up in the archaeological record of the Cape and Namibia are all sheep.

Another picture is drawn by archaeologist John Kinahan on the basis of his work in Namibia. There, the same cultural material pre-dates and post-dates domestic stock, with the exception of pottery, which probably appears with sheep. Kinahan prefers the idea of an indigenous development of pastoralism among local Namibian hunters.

wooded areas.

This was where they first came into contact with hunting people speaking click languages. The archaeology of Zimbabwe shows that the hunting people were in contact with people having domestic stock 2 000 years ago, and most probably by 1 600 years ago the stock farmers were north of the Vaal River and in northern Botswana.

There are several other questions asked by researchers interested in the problem of Khoikhoi origin. Were the herders found at the Cape by early travellers from Europe, immigrants from elsewhere? If they were not immigrants, but local hunting people who had obtained domestic animals, how did the domestic stock get to the Cape? Within these questions lies the more basic question: Do hunters become herders? If so, how? And should the Cape hunters (Soaqua or Sonqua) be seen as different from the Cape Khoikhoi?

To try to find answers, or at least create some likely scenarios, we have to build up the picture from various sources.

The languages of the Cape Khoikhoi and San

Unfortunately no qualified academic linguist was able to study the languages of the people at the Cape before these languages disappeared. But some early travellers and settlers did collect word lists, as aids for other visitors, so we have some clues to the languages spoken. It would appear that the Cape Khoikhoi spoke a dialect of a language also spoken today by Khoe-speaking Bushmen of northern Botswana and Namibia. This language would have been akin to Nama and Koranna, the dialects spoken on the west coast and along the Orange River. This strongly suggests cultural contact between northern Botswana and the Cape. Both Elphick and Ehret suggest that Khoikhoi migrated southwards across the Kalahari to the Orange River with groups moving along the Orange to the west coast, in one direction, and a southward movement along river valleys to the south coast (fig. 9).

Another aspect of the linguistic problem is the relationship between the languages of the Cape Khoikhoi and the Sonqua or Soaqua, or 'Bushmen'. Elphick interprets the historical evidence as suggesting that there was no language difference between the two groups, and uses this as one form of proof that the

Khoikhoi and Soaqua were similar people. The differences lay in losing or gaining stock. In losing stock the Khoikhoi would revert to being hunter–foragers, but once they regained stock by theft, barter or service, they would once more become herders.

Hunters or herders?

In response to Elphick's model, an archaeological project was set up on the Vredenburg Peninsula, north of Saldanha Bay, to see if it was possible to distinguish hunting people from herders. Several sites were excavated, and it became clear that there were indeed two quite distinct groups in the landscape.

One group, found at the large open site of Kasteelberg, had lots of sheep and seal bones associated with large quantities of pottery, large ostrich eggshell beads and grooves in bedrock for grind-

The Elphick cyclical model

Research led historian Richard Elphick to conclude that the difference between Khoikhoi and Soaqua was only one of fortune. He believes that the Khoikhoi economy was rather fragile, since Khoikhoi could easily lose their stock through theft, disease or drought. They would then have to fall back on hunting to survive, and on raiding cattle from other herding groups in order to recoup their losses. Thus he suggested a cyclical model: when a family had domestic animals they would see themselves as Khoikhoi, but when they lost their stock and had to revert to living off *veldkos*, they were seen by stock owners as Soaqua, a reduction in class status.

Figure 11. Elphick's cyclical model.

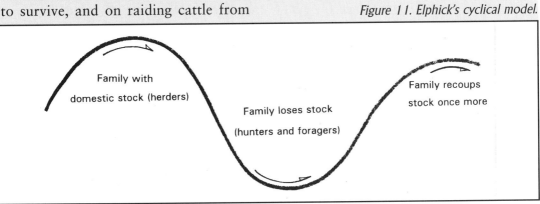

Family with domestic stock (herders)

Family loses stock (hunters and foragers)

Family recoups stock once more

Figure 12. Excavation of the early herder site of Kasteelberg.

ing ochre, but rather crude stone tools.

By contrast, several small rock shelters in the area, including one at Witklip, were investigated. They proved to have been occupied from the period before domestic stock arrived at the Cape until almost the beginning of the colonial era. These sites produced only a few domestic animals in the top layers of the excavation, the bones being dominated by small buck (steenbok in particular).

The cultural material included a few potsherds, tiny ostrich eggshell beads (fig. 13) and finely finished microlithic stone tools. These are tiny stone flakes shaped to make tools which could be used as arrowheads, or for fine woodworking. Almost every aspect of the cultural and economic patterns at the rock shelters differed from those at Kasteelberg.

On the basis of this comparison we can state with a degree of certainty that hunters did indeed differ from herders in the pre-colonial period. The Elphick cyclical model, on the other hand, may be better suited to the period when the colonial expansion of the late 1600s and

early 1700s was putting pressure on the lands and livelihood of the Khoikhoi; it is probable that many of them lost their stock through theft by colonists. In such circumstances, their choice was either to become refugees, joining independent hunting bands for survival, or to become dependent on the growing agricultural economy of the colony as low-status servants to the colonists.

However, archaeologist John Parkington reads the historical literature differently. He suggests that such phrases from writings by early travellers as 'among the Hottentot race there is also one language which all their great ones understand but which the common people do not' indicate that two quite different languages existed, based on social standing. A similar indication of language difference is to be found in the report of Pieter van Meerhoff, who journeyed north of the Cape in 1661, in search of the Namaqua:

> I therefore gave the Souquas drink and tobacco, and spoke with them myself while they were smoking, and they promised to go home and fetch their weapons the same night; they returned

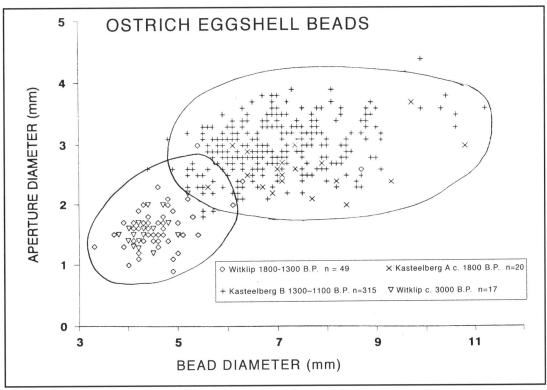

Figure 13. Comparison of sizes of ostrich eggshell beads found in the rock shelters of Witklip and at the herder site of Kasteelberg. In the diagram, the smaller group (to the left) represents the Witlklip beads, while the larger group (to the right) represents those from Kasteelberg.

	KASTEELBERG					WITKLIP		
							1800–	500–
	2100 BP	1800 BP	1300 BP	900 BP	200 BP	3000BP	1400 BP	330 BP
	105/2 78.9%	238/7 7.0%	174/5 3.8%	532/10 6.0%	294/7 8.6%	35/2 53%	162/3 62.5%	26/2 55.3%
	12/2 9.0%	1809/35 53.5%	1332/21 29.2%	1466/23 16.5%	354/10 10.2%	4/1 6.0%	19/2 7.3%	4/1 8.5%
	3/1 6.0%	1218/24 36.0%	2646/30 58.0%	6085/72 65.5%	2391/31 70.0%	3/1 4.5%	1/1 0.4%	

Figure 14. Small ungulates, sheep and seals are the three main animal species whose bones were found at Kasteelberg and Witklip. In the pairs of numbers (e.g. 105/2) the number on the left is the actual number of bones of these animals found; the number on the right is the minimum number of animals represented by these bones. As can be seen, the seal bones dominate the Kasteelberg site, with sheep second most important, while small hunted animals are most common at the Witklip site. This indicates that Kasteelberg was a herder site, but was occupied while people were culling seals at the coast. The Witklip site was occupied by hunting people.

to us at 10 at night, with 4 other Souquas, of whom I had seen 2 on my last journey to the Namaquas; they staid with us, and promised to go, but our Hottentoos held a consultation with them the whole night, about the journey, and Oedasoa and the other Cape Hottentoos. Our interpreter asked them fully 10 times what they were debating about, and they answered, about nothing.

Van Meerhoff probably communicated poorly with the Soaqua, using sign language and some words he had picked up, and so had to rely mostly on Khoikhoi interpreters. But if the interpreters were unable to understand the debate, then even they were not able to communicate adequately at times. Some of the Soaqua may have been bilingual, and so able to talk among themselves in a language unintelligible to the Khoikhoi.

The archaeological sites containing domestic stock are almost always associated with pottery. This means that pottery can be used as a time marker (see 'Dating archaeological remains', p. 6 and fig. 2), but we cannot always be sure that the appearance of pottery on a site means that it was occupied by herders. There are indications that pottery was exchanged between hunting and herding groups, or that a few broken pieces were removed from herding camps by hunters.

Even more confusing is the probability that hunters found domestic stock easy to steal from herders: we often find the bones of sheep or cattle on sites occupied by hunters. What we also find, however, is that the percentages of the different wild and domestic animals vary markedly from site to site. Only small numbers of sheep were found in the excavation at Witklip, whereas Kasteelberg produced considerably more.

We can, therefore, suggest that Kasteelberg was a herders' site, but one from which wild game was also hunted, and that Witklip was a hunters' site. Such a suggestion is supported by the collection of different styles of material goods (such as stone tools and ostrich eggshell beads) on the two sites.

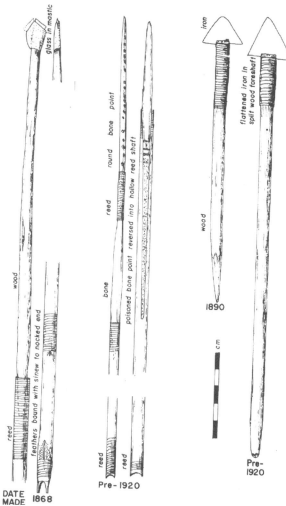

Figure 15. San arrows (those on the left) and Khoikhoi arrows (the two on the right) showing distinct differences in technology and style.

Kasteelberg

Most of the archaeological sites which have produced the bones of domestic animals in the western Cape are caves. Kasteelberg is an important exception. It is a large open-air site among sheltering granite boulders only 4 km from the sea, north of Saldanha Bay. This is the kind of site we would expect to have accommodated families of pastoralists coming together for annual ceremonial activities. The site is 1.7 m deep in places, full of shell, seal and terrestrial mammal bones (e.g. hartebeest, steenbok, sheep,

some cattle and a range of small carnivores such as mongooses). There is some ivory (part of a tusk and a polished bracelet), showing that elephants must have existed in the area.

Excavation has shown that seals are the most important mammal represented – so it was probably a sealing camp, established not so much for meat, but for the fat which could be mixed with ochre and rubbed onto the body as a sign of well-being. Ochre was found throughout the excavation, and many grooves were discovered in the bedrock where ochre had been ground into a powder.

What can we learn about the early herders from Kasteelberg? We have noted that they did not make formally retouched stone tools, but they did make beautifully finished bone points. They used a great deal of red pigment, not only for the outside of their pottery, but mixed with fat to decorate themselves. A description from Van Riebeeck's *Journal*, of Oedasoa, chief of the Cochoqua, shows that in October 1658 this practice still continued: 'like all Hottentots he was dressed in skins and so besmeared that the fat ran down his body, which was the highest mark of distinction'.

The raw ochre was readily available, and fat would have been easily obtained from the many seals represented in the bones from the site. A study, by gas chromatographic analysis, of the residues adhering to the surface of pottery from the site shows that they were marine mammal fats, so the pots were

Figure 16. Grooves in bedrock.
Figure 17. An archaeology student demonstrates how the grooves were made.

21

probably used to render, or boil down, the seal blubber, and perhaps even that of beached whales.

Kasteelberg was first occupied by sheep herders between 1 800 and 1 600 years ago. This is in line with other evidence from Geduld in northern Namibia, Spoegrivier Cave in Namaqualand and De Kelders in the western Cape, which have all produced early dates of between 2 000 and 1 800 years ago for the appearance of herding people.

Figure 18. The archaeological site of Kasteelberg, Western Cape.

Cetacean trap at St Helena Bay

An item of food which is recorded as being used by the Khoikhoi in the records of early colonists and travellers, but which tends to be missing from the archaeological record, is whale meat. The reason why it is 'invisible', archaeologically speaking, is that people would cut meat off the carcass of any stranded whale. Because the bones are so big, they would not be carried back to their camp. The only direct evidence of whales on archaeological sites comes from the appearance of a few barnacles of a species which are parasitic on whale skin, particularly that of the Southern Right Whale. We have to use circumstantial evidence to learn about possible whale use.

Just such evidence is the existence of 'cetacean traps', which are places where whales often strand themselves along the shore. These appear to occur in places where minima in the earth's magnetic field cross the shoreline, and invariably where there are reefs close in off-shore. These conditions are met at Slipper Bay in St Helena Bay, about 12 km from Kasteelberg. Within the last 50 years three major stranding episodes of more than 50 False Killer Whales and dolphins have occurred. These events have happened since whale populations have been reduced by intensive commercial whaling, and so we can assume that stranding would have occurred more often in the past. One explanation for live stranding is that it is linked to whales' guidance systems. Whales seem to respond to the earth's magnetic field when navigating on their migrations. When they accidentally come close in shore, possibly following their prey species of fish or other food, under the conditions outlined above they become disoriented and beach themselves.

Figure 19. Muafangejo's Kraal. *'He had 8 wives, 9 sons, 8 daughters and bushman stayed with us'. John Muafangejo, 1979.*

Hunters and herders

To understand how hunters can become herders we have to look at how they lived. Hunters, as we know from studies of the modern San of the Kalahari, live in small groups. No one owns anything beyond a few personal items, such as tools or clothing. Everything else is shared. They do not build up a surplus of food. Why should they? They gather or hunt what they need for the day's 'pot', and allow the animals and plants to be a living store for them. Domestic stock, to people who do not believe in personal possession of food, is treated just the same way as wild game: immediately slaughtered, shared and eaten.

So how do hunters become herders? The clues to answering this come from attempts to change the economy among some San groups, whose lands are threatened by more powerful people, in Botswana and Namibia today. Such a change is not an easy matter, because of the customary requirement that animals be killed and shared among all members of the camp. A whole new approach is needed to encourage people to think of the future and to conserve the breeding stock. An additional complication is that people with domestic herds are usually reluctant to give away their breeding stock, particularly to people they perceive as being their inferiors. They regard their animals as valuable, not just because they make a person powerful, but because the stock are used in ritual ceremonies as well.

Hunting people living in the vicinity of herding people would probably have performed various services for the cattle farmers, such as looking after stock, providing honey, or being rain-makers. For these services they might be paid in milk and given small stock which would be eaten immediately. Studies of modern San have shown that only those people who have become low-class members of their dominant neighbours' society and have accepted the herding ethos are capable of accumulating and maintaining enough stock to have viable herds. Even then some hunters may simply allow their goats to forage for themselves around the camp while the people go off hunting and gathering. Others look after their animals very carefully, and so stop seeing themselves as hunters, but rather as part of the larger society, even though they have little status within it. In relationships between San and Tswana, San men are unlikely to marry Tswana women because they do not have enough cattle for bridewealth payments. On the other hand, a San woman might marry a Tswana man, and the result is what the physical anthropologist, Alan Morris, calls a one-way gene flow.

The transition from hunting to herding requires a shift in both the social and economic lives of hunting society. Hunters no longer need to share their stock, as the sharing concept is modified and new 'bond friendships' (which rely on mutual giving and receiving) are developed.

How did pastoralism begin in the south-western Cape?

Two possible scenarios can be used to explain the early appearance of domestic animals in the Cape more than 1 600 years ago. The first looks at ways in which animals and pottery were transferred by exchange between various communities living apart from one another, so that the animals are moving, in this case southwards, but without an associated migration of people. The second scenario looks at the possible migration of people, moving with their stock, to colonise new areas.

The first model has been suggested by Kinahan to explain the appearance of stock and pottery in the central Namib Desert around the Brandberg in Namibia. He argues that the stock were introduced by exchange, and that the transition to herding took place as a result of the increasing power of shamans, or religious leaders, to control the community's economy – a situation which Guenther has recognised among the Naron of Botswana. This means they not only had religious power, but gained in political authority and became chiefs. But this still does not explain where the stock originated.

The second model looks further north, and to the transformation of a hunting society to one which produces food. It suggests a movement south by these northern herders with their stock and pottery. In support of this model is the similarity in languages stretching from northern Namibia and Botswana to the Khoikhoi at the Cape. Equally, the pottery from archaeological sites is very similar from Etosha to the Cape south coast. Thus we can make a direct connection between the two areas. Another factor supporting this model is the rapidity with which this dispersion seems to have occurred. Within a hundred years, pottery and stock seem to have been distributed over this large area from northern Namibia to the Cape.

Elphick's idea of an alternative interior migration must also be considered. Crossing the Kalahari could really take place only after an exceptionally good rainy season, when pools of standing water could allow the passage of stock. Elphick suggested a movement to the Orange River, dispersal along it, and southwards along valleys to the coast (fig. 9). Archaeological information from work in the Zeekoe Valley of the Karoo indicates that Khoikhoi occupation of the valley was very late, around the fourteenth century AD, which would tend to rule this out as an earlier migration route.

Around 2 000 years ago a separation of farming people and lower-class herders of small stock may have taken place, possibly in the area north of the Caprivi. Why this may have happened we have no idea, but the effect was that small stock moved across into northern Namibia around 1 800 years ago and spread southwards before 1 600 years ago down the Atlantic coast to the western Cape, where such stock is found on archaeological sites of this date.

Who then were the Khoikhoi?

From these various sources of information we can say that the Khoikhoi were people derived from the aboriginal hunters of southern Africa – most probably, on linguistic grounds, those hunters who lived in northern Botswana. It was possibly in this area that they changed their economy and became herders. They would have had to make significant changes to their social organisation in order to think of themselves as herders – initially as low-class members of a hierarchical agricultural society, and later, once they were separate from the farmers, as independent herders in their own right. Later, along with their herds, they

Rock art showing domestic animals

It is very interesting that only sheep are depicted in the rock art of the western Cape, and this only rarely. The greatest concentration of such images is in the Koebee Valley near Nieuwoudtsville, where the individual sheep sketches comprise 10 per cent of the known paintings in the area. This strongly suggests that the pastoralists were not the painters of the rock art.

In the eastern Cape, paintings of cattle, showing their many different coat colours, have been found. This may be due to the proximity of the black cattle-keepers who were to be found in the grassland areas below the Drakensberg and Winterberg.

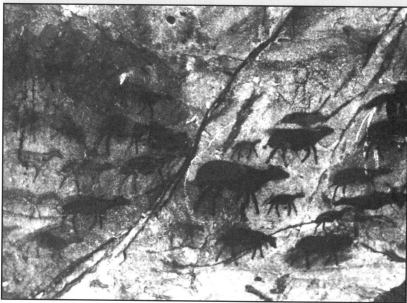

Figure 20 (above). Rock paintings showing cattle, from Brakfontein, Eastern Cape. Figure 21 (left). Fat-tailed sheep in rock art from Boskloof in the Cedarberg, Western Cape.

Figure 22. Khoikhoi herders with a fat-tailed sheep. Artist unknown, early 1700s, SA Library.

probably travelled southwards to the winter rainfall area of the western Cape, and possibly also north of the Vaal. At the time of contact with Europeans, they had large herds of cattle, but these did not exist during the early part of the migration, when all they had were sheep. It is possible that the cattle came from later contact with black African farmers in the eastern Cape.

The spread of nomadic herding is easy to understand, as herders are always on the look-out for pasture and water for their stock. The fat-tailed sheep (fig. 22) they had were ideally suited for crossing the relatively dry areas of Namibia and the north-western Cape to get to the more dependable winter rainfall area of the south-western Cape. These herds, along with their herders, were entering environments already inhabited by San hunters. We must recognise that any introduction of exotic herds is bound to have put pressure on the San's resources, such as grazing for wild game. The incoming herdsmen would have changed the social life and environment of the local hunting population.

The relationship between the two economies was not always peaceable, as we know from historical records, with the San stealing from Khoikhoi herds. On the other hand, there were amicable relations set up when the San worked as clients for the herders, in much the same way as the original herding people had worked for the farmers in the north. The San of the western Cape would have been seen as low-status people, possibly trying to become herders and having the same problems that all hunters do when they try to adapt to keeping stock.

Hunters & herders in the south-western Cape

3

As we have suggested, there were probably two economic groups subsisting side by side in the western Cape before European settlement: hunters and herders.

The coast was very attractive to both groups, because of the marine resources available. In particular, seals were a major focus of attention, as indicated by the high percentage of seal bones at the archaeological site of Kasteelberg. Equally important were shellfish, with large numbers of shells found throughout the deposit. There was probably a division of labour by gender: women would forage for shellfish and plant foods, while men would be concerned with the herds, and with killing seals.

There is an eye-witness account of this happening close to Kasteelberg in October 1653. A French ship's captain reported from St Helena Bay that

> there he had seen the Saldanhars with thousands of cattle and sheep on the plains and spoken to them. He had only been able to barter a few cattle from them, having no copper or tobacco but only small, inferior glass beads. He had also seen Saldanhars at a certain point jutting into the sea [Britannia Point or Duiker Eiland] where they were killing many seals (of which there were thousands) for food.

Figure 23. Khoikhoi herder with his stock. Artist unknown, early 1700s, SA Library.

The excavations at Kasteelberg also give us information about the changing herd structure of the domestic stock. In the early levels only sheep bones are found, but some time before 1 300 years ago cattle were introduced to the site. Since large stock did not come with the herders from Namibia, it is likely that they were acquired through contact with the farming people who had, by this time, reached the limits of the summer rainfall area in the eastern Cape. This natural barrier was important because the crops used by pre-colonial African farmers – sorghum and millet – would not grow in a winter rainfall area, so the farmers did not move further south-west.

Cattle require large amounts of grazing. The western Cape is not a rich grassland environment. Herders introducing cattle to the western Cape would have had to move about with their animals to find enough grazing, especially in summer. For this reason, in that part of their annual grazing cycle which took them inland, the herders are virtually invisible, archaeologically speaking. They moved around so quickly and did not return to exactly the same place every year, and therefore did not leave in one place enough of the garbage that is the evidence archaeologists use.

The ratio of small stock to large stock, calculated on the basis of the bones from Kasteelberg about 900 years ago, was 4.7:1, a herd ratio that is consistent with other pastoral people in Africa. This is a clue to the herd structures that were seen by the Dutch settlers in the 1650s. With the addition of cattle to the herds, there was probably an even greater disparity between the status of large stock owners and those with no stock. This pushed hunters, such as the Soaqua, further onto the far edge of herding society, and made it even more difficult for them ever to become herders in their own right.

Within the herding community stock numbers changed as conditions changed, though numbers were kept within workable limits. Raiding for cattle took place between groups. This was a way in which young men acquired their own herds and established themselves as adults. Disease and drought were also mechanisms of control influencing herd size. But a major limitation was that of labour, the need for men to manage the herds. The usual way for African herdsmen to get round this problem is for them to loan animals out to kinsmen to look after. In this way all the animals are not in a single herd, and the risk of disease or theft is spread. An owner not only can recall his animals if needed, but gets prestige from the patronage of having many people in his debt. The anthropologist Isaac Schapera discusses the concept of *soregus* in Khoikhoi society, 'whereby two individuals, either of the same or of opposite sex, will enter into a specially intimate bond of association [which] implies deep friendship and mutual assistance, especially in economic matters'. Through such bond friendships a man could gain access to breeding stock to recoup stock losses from whatever cause.

As distinct from the hunting and foraging society of the San, where all people are equal, Khoikhoi society was hierarchical. There were rich people, servants (such as the Bergdama, or Damara without stock, in Namibia), and clients who would work as herdsmen as a form of hired labour. A herdsman would receive a young lamb in payment for service.

Ideology and the separation of hunters from herders

We need to understand the ways by which people are kept separate, in order to understand the basis of relationships between different groups of people in South African history.

Figure 24. Khoikhoi with Bushman servant in the nineteenth century.

The Bushmen today

Among the Kalahari !Kung (Bushmen) it has been noted by the psychologist, Richard Katz that

> they are increasingly becoming sedentary serfs and squatters around settlements of Tswana and Herero pastoralists. !Kung families attach themselves to a particular Tswana or Herero family and, in exchange for working their cattle, receive food and a place to build their shelters. Only occasionally do they gather, rarely do they hunt. The *quid pro quo* exchange of services for money, or its equivalent, begins to dominate economic exchanges. The old sharing weakens. These changes in the use of land and the access to land strike at the heart of the !Kung gathering and hunting lifestyle. Private ownership of resources, accumulation of property, cultivation of a piece of land, differential wealth – all signs and mainsprings of capitalism, increasingly evident among the neighbouring pastoralists, threaten to overwhelm the !Kung's present-oriented use of the land, emphasis on sharing and egalitarianism.

Thus the !Kung are very much on the periphery of the dominant society.

At one level, the type of economy of any group is linked with how the group is socially organised, and how many people live together. In San society the numbers are generally small. Camp sizes may vary, depending on the season. Groups of 25 to 50 individuals are most common. In pastoral societies, on the other hand, even though they move around just as much as hunters do, the guarantee of food for many people allows greater group sizes. Having more food than they need – a surplus – also means that the food resources, in this case domestic stock, have value greater than just food. Individuals can control the surplus as wealth. In doing so they can also control the labour of less wealthy people in the society, and so the product takes on symbolic meaning. In herding societies, stock has real symbolic power. The herds become metaphors for the family and important ritual activity revolves around the stock.

Once a group has these symbols of power, political alliances are possible through exchange. In consequence, herding societies are capable of military dominance over hunting–foraging neighbours. This means that stockless people brought into herding society would see themselves – and be regarded by the stock owners – as inferior. Even though the hunters work for the herders, they might be denied access to breeding stock. (Why should the herders want competition?)

Thus class distinctions are possible, with stockless people kept in subservient positions to do work as menials. These same conditions are found today among the San or Basarwa of Botswana, who are placed by Tswana in lower-class positions as stockless people on the land they have used for centuries.

People on the periphery

The process of subjugation and of placing people in inferior positions has a lot to do with making them dependent. People without access to power, or symbols of power such as domestic animals, depend on those who have wealth to give them a portion, but at a price. The price is often servitude. This fixes in place an ideological structure which ensures that the less fortunate accept their position without question. Those who dominate will reinforce this separation by giving symbolic value to material possessions, including livestock. Although individuals may try to improve their status, ideological relations could make it difficult for changes in real social relations to take place.

The concept of 'marginal' people, or people pushed to the edge, was originally developed in an attempt to understand how immigrants were socialised into American culture, and later to deal with the relations between American blacks and the dominant white culture. There were two main aspects to this concept: what the individual thought of his or her position, within both the marginal group and the non-marginal group, and the nature of the barriers separating the two groups. Barriers between social groups are made by those who control resources.

The term 'marginal' is used in various ways to describe different social situations. We wish to use the term in a very specific sense: namely, in all hierarchical societies there are people on the periphery who are excluded from status and access to the important products of the society. These people have a narrow range of choices in making a living and gaining status. The degree to which they are marginalised depends on their ability to find status through their labour, and this, in turn, depends on the numbers of 'surplus people' available to do the work. The greater the numbers, the more marginal will the subordinate group become.

Each individual can consciously make his or her own decisions, as long as there are options open. Conditions get difficult when the options close, increasing dependence and the potential for being pushed even further onto the periphery. In the case of peripheral groups whose social and economic structure is completely different, such as hunters on the edge of a dominant group of herders, alienation can be even greater. This is due to different ways of thinking about work and property, and how these are organised. In such cases the 'barrier' between groups is less 'permeable' or more closed and therefore much more difficult for the subordinate group to cross.

Social relations between Khoikhoi and other groups changed through time. Social conditions can only be looked at in the context of any given moment. It should not be assumed that the historical stereotype of 'the Hottentot' was fixed, or can be generalised. Just as San clients were kept in inferior positions by denying them access to breeding stock, once the Khoikhoi lost their stock and pasture lands to the Dutch colonists they, in turn, were later forced into dependency situations where they had only their labour to offer. The ideology and acceptance of their own power symbols (cattle) were quite firmly fixed. This made it difficult for them to maintain an independent lifestyle, as they were unable to adapt to the colonists' more commercial attitude to stock ownership. Loss of stock forced a change in the way their society was organised and how they controlled their resources had to change, and the Khoikhoi had to accept their status as lower-class menials.

Reconstructing the past

4

The previous chapters have been about the origins of the Khoikhoi – who they were, where they came from, how they came to be herders, and how they related to the hunter society at the Cape. But in order to understand the later history of the Khoikhoi – the way in which they responded to the dramatic changes begun by the settlement of Europeans at the Cape – we need to know more about the pre-existing lifestyle of these herders.

How was their society organised? What was the nature of their political and residential units? What belief system did they have? What was the division of labour between men and women?

These questions are best answered by anthropologists, who study different lifestyles or cultures. But anthropologists know that attempts to reconstruct 'traditional' lifestyles are not without their problems, and we need to look at these problems before we proceed with this chapter.

It is almost impossible to reconstruct the past exactly as it was. This is particularly true in a study of the Khoikhoi, since their culture was so rapidly and completely altered by the arrival of European settlers.

It is wrong to assume that 'traditional' societies did not change at all. While it is

What is social anthropology?

The primary task of social (or cultural) anthropology is to study human social (or cultural) variation. Anthropologists are interested in the variety of ways in which humans have constructed their social worlds in order to deal effectively with basic issues such as the provision of food, procreation, control of material resources, maintenance of order and, very importantly, the interpretation of the world and their place in it.

The origin of social anthropology in the 1800s lay in the reports of strange and exotic peoples produced by travellers, missionaries and colonial administrators. Academic interest in the comparative study of cultures was stimulated. However, after 1900 professional anthropologists became increasingly concerned about the reliability of these second-hand accounts. Many were found guilty of distortion and exaggeration, and of having portrayed the 'other' people as barbaric and primitive.

In response to these concerns, anthropology developed the practice of fieldwork. This is the collection of first-hand data by anthropologists spending lengthy periods amongst the people being studied, learning their language, observing and participating in their everyday lives and conducting interviews. The products of such efforts are referred to as ethnographies and are descriptive accounts of societies or cultures.

Anthropology seeks to describe and understand societies as they exist at the time. But sometimes there is also a need to reconstruct social life as it might have existed before anthropologists arrived on the scene. To do this, anthropologists rely heavily on written accounts and oral history; they also use their knowledge of the way in which other similar societies are organised, to piece together a plausible picture of a social world that no longer exists.

true that the rate of change after European settlement increased rapidly, we cannot assume that the situation in, say, AD 1600 was the same as it was 2 000 years earlier.

Anthropologists today recognise that all societies, even relatively isolated ones such as pre-colonial Khoikhoi society, change as they adapt to, for example, population pressures, climatic variations and contact with other populations. Pre-colonial Khoikhoi were no exception, as they responded to seasonal and longer-term climatic changes, moved around in search of new pastures, re-aligned themselves in different political groupings, and encountered San and Bantu-speak-

ing populations. It is also recognised that other aspects of social organisation are strongly influenced by economic activity. Therefore it is likely that as populations moved around, their dependence on hunting and gathering (as opposed to herding) changed – increasing or decreasing according to circumstance. This must have had a significant impact on political organisation, kinship ties, the sexual division of labour and even on the nature of ritual activity.

Anthropologists trying to reconstruct pre-colonial Khoikhoi life have had to rely heavily on second-hand (and hence often biased and inaccurate) accounts of early travellers or commentators. Or they have had to assume that certain aspects of society have remained relatively constant, in spite of major changes in other domains. For example, are we entitled to assume that Khoikhoi kinship and belief systems have remained relatively intact in the face of the major changes associated with the introduction of wage-labour, incorporation into colonial political structures and conversion to Christianity?

There is also the problem of generalisation. Different herder populations show significant points of cultural variation. For example, there is evidence that tribal units amongst the Cape Khoikhoi (living in the south-western Cape) were much more loosely organised than they were amongst the Nama (in southern Namibia and north-western Cape). Does this variation reflect actual difference, or is it the consequence of different observers and their differing accounts? What of reported differences in inheritance patterns – such as the observation that amongst the Nama the eldest son was the principal heir, while the Cape Khoikhoi divided the inheritance among

Reconstructing the 'traditional' Khoikhoi

By the time the tradition of fieldwork in social anthropology had become established, little remained of Khoikhoi society as it existed before contact with Europeans.

Winifred Hoernlé, generally recognised as the first trained anthropologist to work in South Africa, undertook an arduous trip to north-western Namaqualand in 1912 in search of the 'pure Hottentot' (see *The Richtersveld, the land and its people* (1913) and *Trails in the Thirstland: the anthropological field diaries of Winifred Hoernlé* (1987) edited by P. Carstens, G. Klinghardt and M. West). Even there she was unable to find them, and she was forced to acknowledge that the last traces of traditional Hottentot culture had all but disappeared. Similarly, Isaac Schapera, writing in the 1930s, commented that the various groupings of Hottentots had already 'disappeared' or 'vanished', and that their culture and political organisation had been 'effaced', 'destroyed' or 'hopelessly broken down' (see his clas-

sic, *The Khoisan peoples of southern Africa: Bushmen and Hottentots* (1930)).

Anthropologists interested in Khoikhoi ethnography have had to rely on written reports of early travellers and historians, on detailed and reliable information collected by academics not necessarily trained in anthropology (especially those who study language), and on oral culture, or knowledge about the past in songs, poems and stories passed from generation to generation, to piece together their accounts.

However, Alan Barnard, writing in *The Khoisan people* (1990), argues that there is still work to be done in the reconstruction of traditional Khoikhoi ethnography. He points out that historical sources and oral culture are still able to yield valuable new information and insights. Moreover, he argues that in spite of massive changes in the economic and political spheres, the more resilient aspects of culture, such as kinship and language structures, continue to provide us with new insights into the nature of pre-colonial cultural patterns.

all the children. Could this mean that there were substantial variations in the broad pattern of Khoikhoi society, or could it mean simply that some observers were inattentive to detail, and hence their reports were misleadingly inconsistent? In general, however, various populations of the Khoikhoi showed many cultural similarities. In the account that follows we will try to extract these common themes, rather than look at regional differences.

Finally, there is the problem of writing accounts in a misleading tense. Instead of locating their descriptions in the distant past (as in 'The Khoikhoi *used* to believe in …'), anthropologists have tended to use the present tense (as in 'The Khoikhoi believe in …'). This has served to deny the realities of three hundred years of major social change, particularly during the apartheid era. Anthropologists' accounts of various South African tribes or peoples, written in this way during the 1950s, could be used to argue that the populations in question were 'still locked in the past' – that is traditional, backward or unwilling to change.

Pre-colonial Khoikhoi social organisation

The lifestyle of traditional pastoral societies in Africa is defined by their need to find pasture and water for their livestock. Being constantly on the move orders the social relationships between groups and within the group. While most of the active population may move around for most of the year, there are often people in any group who may not move, such as old people or women with very young children. For this reason, part of the group may split, with the

herders going to where the best pasture is to be found, while the remaining part of the group stays in one place with a few milch cows. They find local, and valuable, food, such as marine shellfish or underground plant foods. They might not see the main herds for several weeks, depending on the season.

The fact that the Khoikhoi were cattle and sheep herders set them apart from the hunting San. This can be used to understand differences in other aspects of their social organisation and culture. For example, a herder economy allowed for higher population concentrations and less need for constant mobility. This in turn affected ideas about the ownership of private property and the way in which rights to land were defined. It is therefore convenient to begin our ethnographic account by looking at Khoikhoi political organisation and residential groups, rights to land, and stock ownership.

Political organisation and rights to land

Unlike the San, who lived in very flexible and mobile bands generally numbering fewer than fifty persons, the village settlement (or kraal) of the Khoikhoi was significantly larger, with often well over one hundred persons.

The basic housing structure was a round hut (*matjieshuis*) made of a frame of green branches planted into the ground and bent over and tied together. This was covered with reed mats. Besides providing a relatively solid dwelling, this structure also had the advantage that it could be dismantled and re-erected in a new location if and when the need arose. Although some of the villages made in this way were relatively permanent, in

The *matjieshuis* (mat house)

Men and women shared the task of constructing the dome-shaped *matjieshuis*. Men cut and planted saplings and tied them together with leather thongs to form a frame. Women had to collect the reeds and manufacture the mats. This was a laborious process which required that each reed be pierced with a series of holes so that they could be threaded together. Women were also responsible for repairing or replacing mats as the need arose.

The *matjieshuis* was well suited to the local environment and to the needs of the Khoikhoi. It was made from materials which were freely available in the whole of the region, and could be easily dismantled and transported. Sometimes the mats were simply removed and rolled up. People left the frames behind if they knew that they would be returning to the same site, or if it was too difficult to transport all the materials.

But the structure also provided very practical accommodation, especially in warmer climates. During warm days it offered a cool, relatively bright shelter, with the crevices between the reeds allowing air to circulate. At the same time, the rounded shape provided protection against strong wind and when it rained the reeds would swell as they absorbed water and so protect against leaks. During very cold months the inside could be lined with skins to offer extra insulation against the elements.

It is hardly surprising, therefore, that the *matjieshuis* was readily adopted by

Figures 25 & 26. Framework and finished matjieshuis.

many of the European farmers who encroached on Khoikhoi territory. In fact, the *matjieshuis* remained, until well into the 1900s, the most common dwelling for descendants of the Khoikhoi in the reserves of Namaqualand (see Chapter 9) and for people of mixed descent and white farmers who did not own land.

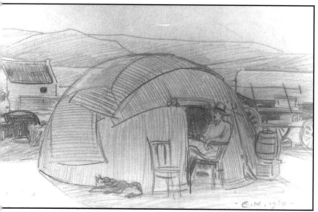

Figure 27. Colonial trekboers quickly recognised the practical advantages of the matjieshuis, *as this sketch by Erich Mayer shows.*

most cases they would have had to be moved every few months as the seasons changed or when grazing in the surrounding area became depleted.

Each village encampment consisted primarily of members of the same patrilineal clan – a group of male descendants of a particular ancestor – with their wives and children. Since a person was not allowed to marry someone of the same clan (we say that such clans were exogamous), men therefore had to find wives from other villages. A man's wife would come to live in his village, while his married sisters would move out to live in their husbands' villages.

Villages generally included some members of other clans, as well as some dependants or servants. These could be Bergdama, San or even impoverished Khoikhoi. Although the village might not include all clan members, as some villages were sections of very large clans, patrilineal descent formed the basis of its social organisation.

Each village recognised the authority of a headman, a hereditary position passed on to the eldest son of the founding ancestor for every generation. Headmen made decisions such as when and where to move. They also acted as the mediator or judge in criminal or civil disputes. There is strong evidence to suggest

Kinship and political organisation: a summary

Different terms have been used to describe the same level of political unit (for example tribe and horde refer to the same thing), and the terms for the political unit and its kinship basis have often been used interchangeably (for example, camp and clan). The following summary may make these relationships easier to understand.

POLITICAL/RESIDENTIAL UNIT	KINSHIP UNITS FORMING THE BASIS OF POLITICAL UNIT	
Matjieshuis/house/hut	Nuclear family	Usually a husband and wife with their unmarried children – but widowed persons, with or without their unmarried children, and single unmarried adults could also have their own houses.
Village/camp/kraal/ encampment	Clan members (and others)	Nearly always more than ten houses, often more than twenty. Between one hundred and several hundred persons of whom the majority were members of a dominant clan. Senior male of dominant clan was headman.
Tribe/horde	Related clans (and other individuals)	Between a few hundred and several thousand people. Up to 15 villages or clans have been reported. Authority of chief recognised.

that headmen were generally the most wealthy stock-owners in the village.

Several villages were usually united into a much larger unit, called a tribe by some or horde by others, which could range in size from a few hundred to several thousand individuals. As with the clan-based villages, tribes had a kinship base. They were made up of a number of linked clans, with the seniority of one of the clans being recognised. In one example, five of seven clans in a tribe were each descended from one of five brothers, with the remaining two being offshoots of these. In this example, the senior clan was the one descended from the eldest brother. The head of the senior clan was recognised as the chief of the tribe.

Local clans could move around and use pasture, water resources, game, and wild fruit and vegetables within the tribal area. Individual clans tended to move in a regular annual pattern in a specific tract of tribal land. Unrelated clans from another tribe, however, had to obtain permission from the local chief to use local resources.

In the areas they occupied, the Khoikhoi herders needed a good water supply above all else, since adequate grazing is of little value without water. Before the arrival of Europeans, the population density was low, which meant that there was little competition for any given piece of land. The extent of tribal land was therefore defined less in terms of exact boundaries than with reference to land around key water-holes.

Tribal chiefs controlled outsiders' access to local resources. Given the variable and often localised rainfall, there must have been a good understanding that herders would often be forced to move temporarily in search of better pastures. It was understood that outsiders could move into another tribal area, as long as they requested permission and paid some form of tribute to the chief. In this way the authority of the chief, and the tribe's established rights to the land, were affirmed. This system showed the flexibility required of nomadic pastoralists in making the best use of available resources. According to at least one botanist's report, dating from the 1700s, the Khoikhoi, by moving around continually, were less destructive of the ecology than Dutch farmers who settled in one area.

The chief 'owned' neither the land nor the resources on it. There was a clear understanding that land could not become the property of individuals, including the chief, and could not therefore be disposed of, in any manner whatsoever, by the chief. The rights granted to outsiders were merely temporary usufruct (users' rights). The tribute given by outsiders acknowledged the tribe's continued rights to the land. This relationship can also be seen as underlining co-operation between the parties, since it was likely that a willingness to share local resources in one area might be repaid in another at a later stage.

Given this understanding of a local tribe's rights to land and its control over it, we can say that the various claims by settlers of having 'purchased' land from local chiefs probably misrepresented the Khoikhoi's understanding of the transaction. They would not have seen this as a 'sale', but as the granting of temporary usufruct, and the 'price' paid would have been seen as the customary tribute.

The common right to land in an area helped to hold the tribe together. This tribal cohesion was further strengthened by the pattern of clan exogamy (marriage outside the clan) and by the many links between the chief and the various villages.

Men from one clan had to seek wives in another. Because related clans within the tribe were geographically close to one another, it is likely that most men found wives within the tribe. And marriage, as is so often the case worldwide, can serve as a very powerful social mechanism to unite different groups. Among the Khoikhoi the custom was that the bridegroom had to spend the first months of marriage (usually until the birth of the couple's first child) living at the village of his parents-in-law. The wife, of course, was expected to spend the rest of her marriage in the village of her husband. In this way strong social links were maintained between the various clans in the tribe.

As leader of the tribe, the chief had a uniting influence on all its members. But there were also other ways in which links between the chief (and his village) and tribal members were promoted.

The chief was acknowledged to be the head of the tribe and could, through individual ability and effort, command a great deal of authority and respect. But he still remained dependent on the wishes of the tribal council. The council consisted of the headmen of all the other clans. The chief could not do much without their support. He and his council would also act as a court in settling various civil disputes and in giving judgment in certain criminal cases.

The council served as a body which linked the various clans together. Such links were further strengthened in those tribes where the older members of the various clans would act as clan 'representatives' and live permanently at the main tribal 'headquarters', the village of the senior clan.

Nevertheless, while there were mechanisms for promoting order and links within the tribe, this did not mean that the tribe's external boundaries always remained in one place, or that the tribe was a more important political unit than the clan.

Marriage links between different tribes were not uncommon, where tribes were geographically close enough to permit this, and tribes were known to co-operate against a common enemy. We have also seen how members of another tribe could be granted permission to use local resources. It was possible to cross both social and geographical boundaries.

It is also important to mention that tribes, as social units, were fluid. They could change in response to changing situations, especially the need for land. For example, when a particular clan became very large, it could split to form new clans within the tribe, or it might even move out of the area. Elsewhere it might assert its independence, ultimately becoming a new tribe. Such episodes appear to have been very common, and probably account for the difficulty some European writers had in deciding whether they were dealing with a clan or an autonomous tribe. It also supports the common assertion that, in spite of the existence of tribes, the clan remained the strongest political unit of the Khoikhoi.

Stock ownership and management

Although the Khoikhoi are generally known as herders or pastoralists, food obtained by hunting and gathering formed an important part of their diet. Wild animals provided the greater part of their meat supply. They usually slaughtered domestic stock for food only on festive and ceremonial occasions.

Their methods of hunting and associated social practices, such as the sharing of meat, were much the same as those found amongst the San. But there were some differences which show that, although hunting was an important economic activity, pastoralism was an integral part of Khoi society. For example, there are reports that a sheep or goat was slaughtered when a hunter killed a very large animal, such as an elephant, rhinoceros or hippopotamus. Similarly, it was noted that in some tribes a portion of the kill from hunting had to be given to the chief, on the understanding that wild animals were part of his 'herd'.

The sharing of food was an important aspect of village life. Any significant kill was shared, and sheep or cattle killed during ceremonial feasts were eaten by all present. Although wealth was measured in terms of livestock ownership, hunting and gathering were activities open to all members of the tribe.

The Khoikhoi kept large herds of fat-tailed sheep, long-horned cattle, and goats. Livestock were used for their milk (sheep and goats included) and were generally slaughtered only on ritual occasions. Oxen were used as pack animals, especially when camp was moved, and were also ridden. A piece of wood, bone or leather through the nose served as attachment for the bridle.

All stock were individually owned, and a wealthy stock-owner was accorded high status. Some individuals, especially chiefs and headmen, owned a large number of stock. One such chief was reported to have 4 000 head of cattle and 3 000 sheep. On the other hand, many individuals, such as servants and other dependants, owned no stock whatsoever. But while individuals clearly sought to maximise their herds, there were various social mechanisms whereby inequalities could be accommodated and poor people could acquire livestock, as we shall see.

The daily routine in the kraal was, as far as we can ascertain, relatively unhurried and leisurely (except when they were moving to a new location, or during the lambing season). Cattle were left to roam freely. They needed no protection from predators and, since kraals were always located near a water source, they returned of their own accord every evening. Sheep, goats and young calves, on the other hand, required close supervision, and young boys, or herdsmen in the employ of the wealthier stock-owners, were given the task of herding them. The herds would be taken out every day in search of grazing, and usually returned to the kraal at night. As grazing became scarce, however, the herdsmen (or boys) might establish stockposts away from the kraal, or the kraal might even move away for a while.

During the day the adults might have remained at the kraal, occupying themselves with the manufacture of utensils and weapons, or with domestic chores. More commonly, however, the men spent their days hunting and the women gathering *veldkos* (wild plant foods).

Many villages included impoverished people who owned few or no livestock. There were individual 'servants' who were attached to wealthy households, where they received subsistence in return for performing tasks. The men acted as herdsmen and women did menial domestic chores. It was also customary for the adult men of poorer households to enter into relationships with wealthy stock-owners. In return for caring for the herd they had free access to the milk, and it was also common for them (usually after some length of service) to receive payment, either in the form of an agreed number of livestock, or by sharing the increase of the herd with the owner.

In this way it was possible, at least in theory, for poor households to acquire stock and eventually to build up substantial herds of their own. In practice, however, it seems to have been very difficult. Cattle were difficult to obtain as payment for services rendered, since, as a rule, they were not herded. Written accounts always specify payment in the form of sheep or goats. We also know that herdsmen generally stayed with their masters for life, which suggests that their own herds rarely grew big enough for their households. The manufacture and trade in household goods and weapons offered another, limited opportunity for economic advancement.

Poorer people had little real chance to build up large herds. This helps us to understand why so many Khoikhoi readily responded to the opportunities for wage employment that the European settlers created.

In most cases wealthier stock-owners acquired their stock by inheritance. In some tribes the inheritance was shared amongst all the children. In others, only sons inherited. In yet others, the eldest son was the only heir. But inheritance after the father's death was by no means the only way in which stock were transferred from one generation to the next. It was common practice for a man to set aside particular stock from time to time for each of his children. These animals became the property of the individual son or daughter, even though they might remain part of the father's herd. They were not included in the deceased's estate. Sons setting up their own herds, and daughters who married, were entitled to remove their own livestock before their father's death.

In this way, children developed an interest in the welfare and management of the family herd. Women and girls milked the cows, and married women took part when decisions regarding the management of the herd were made. But it also meant that certain families held large herds of livestock from one generation to the next. There was a wide gap between wealthy stock-owners and those who owned few or no livestock. Poor families, as measured in livestock ownership, were looked down upon, whether they were San or Khoikhoi.

There was probably a strict division of labour among the Khoikhoi, with cattle being men's work and women and children looking after the small stock. This is suggested in the traveller Thunberg's description of the Khoikhoi in 1775:

> The men use likewise cow's milk, which they milk themselves, and the women sheep's milk ... The men's business is to go to war, hunt, milk, kill the cattle and fabricate arms; the women's, to look after the children, fetch wood, dig up

Figure 28. Khoikhoi milking. Artist unknown, early 1700s, SA Library.

bulbous roots, and dress the victuals [prepare the food]'.

What is not clear from Thunberg's description is how much control women had over the distribution of milk and meat once it was in their hands. We can, however, look at Beaman's description of the pastoral society of the Rendille in northern Kenya:

> On the hoof, the livestock belongs to men. But as soon as the milk is delivered to the wife, she is in control of its distribution ... Likewise, any animal that is killed passes into the hands of the wife. Women may not kill animals but they are responsible for butchering and distribution.

Ritual and everyday life

Religious beliefs and practices are an important part of any society. The comparative study of different religions has been a fruitful field of anthropology. But anthropologists are not simply interested in documenting the variety of exotic religious beliefs and practices 'because they are there'. Underlying much of our interest in religion is an attempt to under-

stand why people behave as they do. Ritual behaviour – especially formal ceremonies and the deliberate use of symbols, and the beliefs associated with them – helps us to understand other aspects of society. Religion can be seen as an extension or reflection of society in general.

In many societies there is, for example, a cult of the ancestors – a strong belief in the power of dead relatives to influence the lives of their descendants. This underlines the importance of descent groups in these societies, and reinforces the way these groups bond together and the authority given to their senior (living) members.

The central theme of almost all Khoikhoi ritual was the idea of transformation, or transition from one state to another. Most rituals marked the critical periods of change in a person's life – birth, puberty, adulthood, marriage and death. Following the work of the anthropologist Van Gennep, we refer to such rituals as 'transition rituals', 'life-crisis rituals' or 'rites of passage'.

It appears that the Khoikhoi not only

practised transition rites, but that they also clearly recognised the social function of such rituals. The Khoikhoi concept of !nau refers to a particular state, of vulnerability or danger, associated with the person undergoing the transition. Some early writers, notably Kolb and Gordon, translate !nau as 'andersmachen' or 'andersmaaken', a verb meaning 'to make different, or to transform', suggesting that the Khoikhoi consciously understood the social process involved in such rituals.

The ritual and festive activity which took place when a child was born often recurred in other Khoikhoi rituals. Just prior to delivery, the mother-to-be was taken to a hut where she remained for at least seven days after the delivery. Both she and the child were seen to be vulnerable and so certain avoidances were practised. For example, no men – not even the husband – were allowed to enter the hut. The mother and baby had to avoid inessential contact with water (especially cold water). For the first three days the baby was not permitted mother's milk and was fed, instead, on milk from goats or cows. At the same time, certain protective practices, such as the lighting of a special fire in the hut, were in evidence.

After this period of seclusion the mother and the father were ceremonially reintroduced into society. Their bodies were smeared with cowdung, fat and buchu, a fragrant plant. The child was also, but not necessarily at the same time, rubbed with a range of substances and introduced for the first time to water. Finally, these rituals of incorporation (or reincorporation) into society were accompanied by a feast in which members of the kraal and blood-relatives from other kraals participated.

Marriage ceremonies, which always seem to have taken place at the home of the bride's parents, also involved a period of seclusion, certain avoidances, and some process of affirmation of the couple's married status. Cattle were given to the mother-in-law, and sometimes the father-in-law also, by the bridegroom, in recognition for having raised his bride. And the groom also had to provide for the feast that followed. But, in general, participants were not seen to be too vulnerable or at risk, and so the avoidances and other protective measures were not very elaborate.

On the other hand, remarriage ceremonies, where one or both partners had been married previously, were seen to be very problematic and extra rituals were added to the ceremony described above. After the regular marriage feast, a special remarriage feast was held. The bride and groom were taken to a hut which had been specially built for them, and, since they were considered to be particularly vulnerable and potentially dangerous to others, no one who had not gone through the same ceremony was permitted to enter. An old woman, who had herself gone through the remarriage ceremony, presided over a ritual during which incisions were made in the bodies of the bride and groom, and blood of a specially slaughtered sheep or goat, mixed with various other substances, was rubbed into the cuts. The couple was then held together so that their blood could mix. Only then could others enter the hut. The slaughtered animal could be eaten only by people who had undergone the same ceremony.

Once the wounds had healed completely the couple were reintroduced to everyday life: their bodies were smeared and cleaned, a completely new set of clothes replaced their old, and both were ceremonially reintroduced to their respective chores (milking, fetching water, cooking and collecting firewood, caring for the cattle). Both were also reintroduced to water, which they had been forbidden to touch while in the hut.

Khoikhoi ceremonies all involved a period of seclusion associated with vulnerability and danger. During these periods of social withdrawal certain things, notably water, were avoided, while others, such as fire and buchu, were associated with protection. The ceremonies also involved a clear process of reincorporation into society, but as persons with new roles.

What is also interesting is the part played by livestock; not only in feasting, but in the ceremonies themselves. In contrast to water, domestic stock seem always to have been associated with protection. This is evident from several ritual practices: feeding babies with milk from cows or goats, rubbing sheep's blood into the incisions of a remarrying couple, and wearing parts of slaughtered animals, as in the case of female puberty rituals.

During initiation ceremonies, stock were ceremonially killed, and as Engelbrecht has described:

> The omental fat (that connecting the stomach with other viscera) was pounded and mixed with red ochre, and this mixture they rubbed into the body of the candidate. Until the period of seclusion was at an end he would always be covered with this ochre and fat.

Figure 29. A pre-colonial skeleton, dated to about 1 000 years ago, was found in the Cobern Street excavations in Cape Town, under the direction of Alan Morris of the University of Cape Town in 1995. The body had been buried in a sitting position, with the knees up to the chin. This skeleton was placed in the grave on top of an earlier one, which had a whole pot associated with it. The combination of pottery and grindstones covering the grave shaft indicates that these were Khoikhoi burials.

The omentum, part of the animal's intestine, was often hung around the neck of individuals to show that they were going through change or transition. For example, Mentzel noted in 1782 that at a funeral:

> the heir slaughters a sheep and the nearest relatives do likewise. The meat is shared by all the inhabitants of the kraal. A gut of the sheep slaughtered by

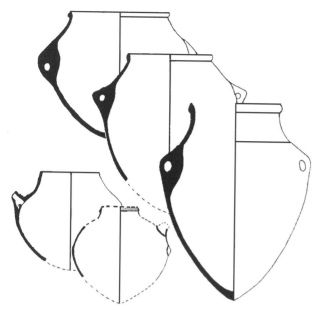

Figure 30. Herder pottery as reconstructed from fragments found at archaeological sites.

the heir is cleaned, richly bestrewed with buchu, and fastened round his neck. This is his sign of mourning, and he is obliged to wear it until it breaks of its own accord and drops down as decayed matter. He does this very willingly, and looks after it as carefully as possible, imagining that otherwise the deceased would return and torment him. The other relatives do likewise with the intestines of the sheep they had slaughtered, and given for the funeral feast.

All of this points not only to the importance of pastoralism in the lives of the Khoikhoi, but also to their long association with domestic livestock. The fact that livestock were almost never slaughtered except on ritual occasions shows a high regard for their breeding stock, and a long-term view of the value of domestic herds. It also raises some questions about the ability of poorer families (those with no or very few stock) to enter

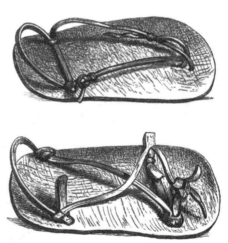

Figure 31. Khoikhoi sandals. Skins were manufactured into clothing, footwear, bags and blankets. Reeds were threaded together to make sleeping mats. The Khoikhoi also made pottery, some of which had distinctive pointed bases and handles (lugs) which could be tied to their oxen when moving, or to hut poles. They made spears (assegais) with fire-hardened tips, but generally used iron tips, which they obtained from neighbouring Bantu-speaking peoples or, later on, from European ships and settlers.

Figure 32 (left). Fat storage container of the Namaqua.
Figure 33 (above and right). Wooden vessels and knife, and Namaqua wooden bowl. The Khoikhoi used mainly wooden and leather material. Any basketry and iron most probably came from contact with black African farmers.

fully into the established ranks of Khoikhoi society.

The rituals also tell us something about social relationships and status in Khoikhoi society. Wealthy stock-owners gained prestige by their ability to provide stock for the feasts they hosted. Marriage involved the transfer of cattle from the groom's family to the parents of the bride, and there are some reports that the bride's parents provided a dowry (in the form of livestock) to the couple. Such public transfers of wealth could also emphasise the prestige of the parties involved, and probably also served to ensure that most marriages were between persons of similar status.

The emphasis on transition rituals to mark an individual's change in status shows us clearly how important age was in defining status in Khoikhoi society.

This emphasis on age can also be found in kinship terms used by Khoikhoi communities. Specific terms were used to refer to older or younger siblings. There were even specific terms to differentiate maternal aunts who were older from those younger than the mother.

The sexes were separated, and men and women had different tasks in ceremonies. This matched the sexual division of labour in Khoikhoi society. However, the central role played by women in the various ceremonies highlights the fact that women exercised considerable power within the household. Women could own stock in their own right, and in some cases became regents or temporary chiefs.

An awareness of the way in which cattle were a part of the social and political life of Khoikhoi society is crucial to

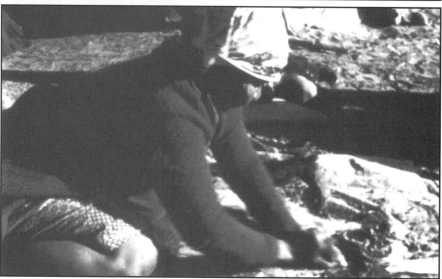

Figure 34. Namaqualand, 1987. Sanna Dirks uses a stone to make an abrasive gravel (left) for the preparation of skins (below).

understanding the differences in world-view between Khoikhoi and Dutch. These differences ultimately proved fatal to Khoikhoi economic life. To the Khoikhoi, cattle were not seen as a product. They were not something that was bought and sold. They had ritual and social significance far beyond monetary value.

The Dutch, on the other hand, saw all livestock as part of the general merchant capital being used to keep the colony in operation. Once the Khoikhoi started to trade some of their stock, the Dutch thought that they were making their cattle a product to be bought and sold. But the Khoikhoi did not see the sale of non-breeding stock in this way. This set up a contradiction within the trading partnership, with neither side really understanding the other. As long as cattle were 'family' and the Khoi had enough stock to maintain their traditional lifestyle, there was no problem. However, as a result of theft, coercion and non-productive exchange (livestock for alcohol, copper, beads, etc.) loss of stock produced a downward spiral that the Khoikhoi could not break. It is what is referred to today as the 'poverty or deprivation trap' affecting large parts of the Third World. The breakdown in the social and eco-nomic values of the Khoikhoi went hand in hand with greater dependency. This is seen in the increasing reliance by the Khoikhoi on the Dutch as mediators in disputes, and in growing Dutch interfer-ence in the raiding patterns between groups of Khoikhoi.

Religion and nature

The Khoikhoi attached a special signifi-cance to the moon, but it is probably incorrect to assume, as some ethnogra-phers have done, that it was 'wor-shipped'. Although new moon and full moon were important times for rain-making rites and dancing, it seems that the moon was merely the physical mani-festation of a supreme being associated with heaven, earth and especially rain (of key significance to people in drier regions, whose existence was so depen-dent upon rainfall).

Amongst the Nama two prominent figures stand out in their religious mythology. The first is *Tsui-//goab*, the deity who was sometimes seen as the founding ancestor of the Khoikhoi. He was 'the creator, the guardian of health, the source of prosperity and abundance, and above all the controller of the rain and its associated phenomena of clouds, thunder and lightning'. By contrast, *//Gaunab* was 'primarily an evil being, who causes sickness or death'. The other major figure is *Haitsi-aibib*, a folk hero and magician of great repute who could change his form. *Haitsi-aibib* died many times in different places, but had the ability to come to life again – often being reborn in a different form. His 'graves' are widely distributed, and it was (and still is) seen as good luck for passers-by to add to the piles of stones already there, or to leave branches, pieces of their clothing, or skins.

For the Khoikhoi the year started with the rains in August. They also had names for other times of the year, which approximate to our calendar months as follows:

August	≠ha!am	broad green (rains, grass and flowers)
September	Xoub/gu//khab	shit moon[1]
October	(hoo)[2]≠gais	speckled ear (veld begins to dry)
November	!kani//khab	eland's moon (eland mating month)
December	/ga!kani	little eland
January	kei!kani	great eland
February	(ong)[2]//o-ha	star death
March	!hoa≠gais	twisted ears (dassies have young)
April	gama/ais	crooked fire (hungry period)
May	≠nu//khab	black moon (grass begins to grow)
June	//hei//khab	pale moon (good grass, flowers start)
July	//gai/ab	chewing wood (becoming cold)

1 The large quantities of milk drunk by the Khoikhoi in this month would markedly affect the appearance of human faeces.
2 Transcribed from Gordon's 1779 notes on the Khoikhoi.

Raiding

Van Riebeeck's *Journal* makes it clear that strained relations existed between different Khoikhoi groups, and that raiding between them took place on a regular basis. There are several reasons why African pastoralists raided each other. At one level, according to the studies of Fukui and Turton, all herders share a 'high social evaluation of cattle and more-or-less severe environmental constraints which call for mobility, physical endurance and highly developed 'bush skills' from the herders'. Raiding by young men fosters these skills. From a successful raid, herds are enlarged and status is raised. The labour needs of herding societies severely limits the size of the herd, and if, after a raid, the herd is too big to be looked after properly, reprisal raids may result in loss. Raiding and counter-raiding allowed for a balance to be reached between the needs of a group and its ability to manage the herd.

Raiding was an integral part of the social reproductive process of all pastoral people in Africa, but raiding hostilities were controlled by certain conventions. If some of the rules were broken (the raids might become too frequent, too many cattle might be taken, or the abduction of young girls might become excessive), then full-scale warfare could be averted by compensation and negotiation. When raiding was prohibited by the French after their defeat of the camel-herding Tuareg of the Sahara in 1902, this undermined the psychological and moral dynamism of the whole society.

The Dutch at the Cape were asked to act as intermediaries and protectors during the first decade of the colony. Van Riebeeck's *Journal* recorded incidents such as this, on 14 July 1656:

> a large troop of Hottentots ... came with many head of cattle ... and were now being chased by the Soanqua ... They accordingly asked to be allowed to encamp under the protection of our fortress.

And on 30 November 1661:

> Early this morning the chief of the Gorachouquas, Choro, with his brother and 3 of their headmen, came to the fort, escorted by one of our frontier guards. They brought with them 6 head of cattle as a present, and requested that we should protect them against the Cochaquas.

But, as Richard Elphick has pointed out, it wasn't until the 1670s that the Dutch East India Company began to assume the right to mediate between Khoikhoi groups:

> Before that time virtually all Khoikhoi had been regarded as members of independent tribes, and if the Dutch interfered in their tribal affairs (as they rarely did) they did so as an act of 'foreign policy' without appeal to the laws of the Cape settlement. But in 1672 the Council of Justice passed judgement in two cases involving Khoikhoi, thus establishing their jurisdiction.

This juridical interference in Khoikhoi affairs increased, as can be seen in the following events of 23 December 1676:

> A certain Hottentot captain named Jacob ... received from us 1 cow and 3 calves ... came to complain to us a few days ago that the animals had been taken away from him by Captain Schacher and his people. We ... imprisoned two of Schacher's Hottentots until he comes to inform us what induced

him to act as he has done.

Since stock theft was a way of life, the Khoikhoi would in earlier times have dealt with the problem on their own terms. Now we see the settlement being asked to adjudicate. Two days later,

> The Hottentoo Schacher ... replied that he had never yet done anything against the Company and as he had returned the cattle he begged that we might forgive him. To this we consented, and thereupon the African left.

Captain Schacher was involved in a similar dispute in February 1677. The outcome was that 'at the recommendation of the Governor they arranged the whole in an amicable manner, and promised that should any of them be again injured by another, he would first communicate the same to us, before taking revenge'.

In less than 25 years of the colony's existence we see the gradual dependence of the Khoikhoi on the Dutch as arbiters. This implies greater economic and social control over the herders. By interfering in raiding between groups, the Dutch were not only setting themselves up as arbiters, but were undermining the authority of the Khoikhoi leaders. What was perhaps even more important, was that they were interfering in a major symbolic act of manhood, possibly placing the elders in conflict with the young men. A direct consequence of this would have been Khoikhoi emigration away from the Cape and Dutch influence.

Khoikhoi & San before European settlement

5

The written record of Khoikhoi contact with Europeans begins with the account by João de Barros, a Portuguese historian writing in the 1500s who described Bartolomeu Dias's attempt to establish a sea route around Africa to Asia in 1487–8. After rounding the southern cape which they called 'Tormentoso' (later renamed 'Spes Bona' or Good Hope) the voyagers reached a point near Mossel Bay

> which we called the Angra dos Vaqueiros, because of the many cows seen there, watched by their herdsmen. And since they had no language which could be understood, we could have no speech with them; but rather they drove off their cattle inland, as if terrified at such a new matter, so that we could learn no more of them than they were blacks, with woolly hair like those of Guinea.

This account does not mention an incident known to later mariners: in 1497, Vasco da Gama's diarist, probably Alvaro Velho, 'marvelled greatly' at the trusting way the Mossel Bay herders approached the Portuguese,

> for when Bartolomeu Dias was here they fled from him, and would not take from him anything that he offered them; but rather, one day as he was tak-

"I think we might give Africa do Sul a miss, Capitao Bartolomeu ... Too much bloody politics."

Figure 35. In 1988 some people opposed the celebrations to mark the quincentenary of the Dias landing at Mossel Bay. A cartoonist transposed these protests to 1488, to suggest how history might have been changed. (Grogan, Cape Times, 18 January 1988).

ing in water from a very good watering-place that lies at the edge of the sea here, they defended this watering-place with stones thrown from the top of a hillock which is above it; and Bartolomeu Dias fired a crossbow at them, killing one of them.

The reaction of the Khoikhoi to Dias helping himself to water in the quotation above tells us that they considered the water belonged to them. This is a common feature of pastoral people in Africa, where water-holes are 'owned' by the group which maintains them to keep them open. Permission for others to use the water is usually granted if it is politely requested, and a gift given. The Portuguese were just ill-mannered 'barbarians', as far as the Khoikhoi were concerned. This brings us to an important point. The Khoikhoi were treating the Europeans just as they would other Khoikhoi – as equals. In contrast, many of the European travellers looked down upon the Khoikhoi as 'savages' because they were

entirely naked but for an ox-hide around them like a cloak ... always stank greatly, since they besmeared themselves with fat and grease ... begged for entrails, which they ate quite raw after scraping out most of the dung, or stretched it over the fire in four sticks ... they speak very clumsily, like the folk in Germany who suffer from goitre.

They were also deemed so ignorant of European values that they traded 'an ox for two knives, a sterk [calf] for a knife and a sheepe for a knife; and some … for lesse value than a knife.'

It seems unlikely that the Europeans, many of whom must have come from an agricultural background, were unaware of the implications of poaching from the herders' water supply. The fact that they 'could have no speech' did not make negotiation impossible, had their first wish been for good relations and the preservation of peace. Whatever they 'offered' as compensation, the explorers' wants – in this case, water – placed them in contention with the pastoralists. We don't know exactly what happened, but we do know the outcome: filled water casks for the Portuguese and a Khoikhoi corpse on the beach.

Before he met these herders, da Gama found people who were almost certainly San at St Helena Bay. The encounter (see box) began with an abduction and ended with a fight. But we also read details of physical appearance including dress and ornamentation, weaponry, the exploitation of available foods, the San's readiness to barter, the presence of domestic

Da Gama's diary: the San at St Helena Bay

On Tuesday [7 November 1497] we … had sight of … a great bay … To this bay they gave the name of Sta Ellena. On Wednesday we cast anchor in said bay; and here we remained for eight days, cleaning the ships, repairing the sails and taking in firewood … In the land the men are swarthy. They eat only sea-wolves [seals] and whales and the flesh of gazelles and the roots of plants. They wear sheaths on their members. Their arms are staffs of wild olive trees tipped with fire-hardened horns. They have many dogs like those of Portugal, which bark as do those … the land is very healthy and temperate, and has good herbage.

On the next day after we had come to rest here … we went ashore with the Commander, and captured one of those men. He was small of body, and … was going about gathering honey on the moor … We took him to the Commander's ship, who placed him with himself at his table, and he ate of everything that we ate. The next day the Commander clothed him very well and ordered him to be put ashore. On the following day fourteen or fifteen of the men came to where we had our ships. The Commander went ashore, and showed them many goods, to learn if there were any of those things in that land, and the goods were cinnamon and cloves and seedpearls and gold, and other things also; and they did not know those goods at all … And the Commander accordingly gave them little bells and rings of pewter.

This was on Friday; and the same happened on the Saturday following. And on Sunday there came about forty or fifty of them … we went ashore, and with çeitis [small copper coins] … we bartered for shells that they wore in their ears, which looked as if they had been silvered over; and for fox-tails, which they carry fastened to sticks, and with which they fan their faces. Here I bartered a sheath which one of them wore on his member, for a çeitil. From this it seemed to us that they prized copper; and they also wore small beads of it in their ears. The same day one Fernão Veloso ... begged the Commander for the favour of permission to go with them to their dwellings. And the Commander ... allowed him to go ... and he went with the said blacks. Soon after leaving us they caught a sea-wolf; and they went to the foot of a hillock on the moor and roasted it, and gave some of it, and some of the roots of plants which they eat, to Fernão Veloso ... When eating was finished, they told him that he must return to the ship, and that they did not wish him to go further with them.

And the said Fernão Veloso, as soon as he came opposite the ships, began to shout, while the men remained concealed in the brushwood. We were still at supper; but as soon as we heard him we put ourselves into the sail-boat. The blacks began to run along the beach; and they came as near to Fernão Veloso as we were. When we were about to pick him up they began to attack us with assegais ... wounding the Commander and three or four men.

dogs, the range of trade goods, and the terrain and climate.

Other accounts of the skirmish maintain that the blacks meant no harm, only hurling their assegais when they believed that da Gama and his landing party intended an attack. According to these writers, da Gama took revenge with crossbows once his men were safely back on board their ships.

Shortly after da Gama reached Mossel Bay, 'there arrived about ninety men, swarthy of appearance like those of Sta Ellena Bay ... and when we saw them we went ashore in the boats, which we armed very well'. It was these men who amazed the diarist by coming close and taking from da Gama's hand some 'little bells'. Still, da Gama decided against a landing at that spot because of 'a great thicket where the blacks were', and went ashore at a 'more open place' with well-armed men. Permitting only one or two Khoikhoi to approach, da Gama 'gave little bells and red caps, and they gave us ivory bracelets which they were wearing on their arms'.

Saturday, 2 December 1497, may be significant as the day when the livestock trade between Khoikhoi and European began. According to Alvaro Velho, men arrived 'bringing with them about twelve cattle, oxen and cows, and four or five sheep; and when we saw them we went ashore at once'. The Europeans were impressed by the large, 'very marvellously fat, and very tame' oxen which they saw: 'they are gelded, and some ... have no horns. And the blacks fit the fattest of them with pack-saddles made of reeds ... and on top of these some sticks to serve as litters, and on these they ride.' The sheep were also very fat. Everyone was in a celebratory mood. The Khoikhoi

> at once began to play on four or five flutes, and some of them played high and others played low, harmonising together very well for blacks from whom music is not to be expected; and they danced like blacks. The commander ordered trumpets to be played, and we in the boats danced, and so did the Commander when he again came to us. When this festivity was ended we went

Figure 36. Khoikhoi women dancing. The artist's sketch for this drawing originally included some musical notation. Possibly 'de toon van dans' noted there was played on flutes like the ones heard by Vasco da Gama and his crew in 1497. Artist unknown, early 1700s, SA Library.

ashore where we had been before, and there we bartered a black ox for three bracelets. We dined off this on Sunday; and it was very fat, and the flesh was as savoury as that of Portugal.

But here de Barros, the historian, writes a totally different account: if these festivities took place, they were not inspired by barter for fat oxen, since 'of cattle we could never have even one head, because they so greatly esteemed them'. This is easy to believe, for, in general, the Khoikhoi were to show great reluctance to part with their good animals. However, Barros had not been present himself.

After several days, some women and small children appeared, although they kept their distance from the Portuguese while the men came to talk. It was thought that the men would barter, until they 'pointed at the watering-place, asking why we took their water; and they began to drive their oxen towards the bushes'. This was seen as the start of 'treachery', so the Portuguese put on their breast-plates and armed themselves, 'rather to show that we were powerful than to do them harm, for this we did not wish to do'. But when they fired two small cannon, the Khoikhoi, who were all now seated on the beach, fled in terror, throwing down their clothes and weapons as they ran. The voyagers continued to take water.

On their last day ashore, they filled more water casks. They also erected a pillar ('padrão') and a cross made from a mizzenmast. But as they prepared to leave the bay, they 'saw some ten or twelve blacks who threw down both the cross and the padrão before we sailed'. Apparently da Gama returned to Mossel Bay on his way home in 1499, but aside from the claim that a Mass was said there, nothing else is known.

These first encounters show how problems of communication harmed relations between the herders and the Portuguese. Uncertainties concerning loss and gain, as well as fear of the unknown, perplexed both sides. If the Portuguese had had more respect for the rights of the native inhabitants of the

Interpreting the historical record

The pool of information we call history comes mainly from written records which have been preserved in archives and libraries. Historians write about what these records contain, enabling the rest of us to understand how people lived and what they thought and why they acted the way they did. In days gone by, if two historians wrote conflicting versions of the same event, then it was likely to be claimed that one or both were 'biased'. 'Bias' occurred when writers failed to be 'objective'.

We see the problem differently today. Historians may strive to be objective but, like other people, they tend to view the evidence before them in terms of the environment in which they live and the values which they hold. The written records are not waiting for a perfectly objective historian who will tell us, finally, what they mean. They are resources: new questions will yield new information and analyses which challenge our ideas.

Another problem for historians concerns their power to influence the way people perceive those outside their own group. Western historians in the 1800s unashamedly fostered pride in the achievements of their 'own kind'. To show that those outside were backward or savage they relied on written records which described societies that, often, they had never seen. They interpreted these accounts in terms of social and scientific theories which were popular at the time. Intentionally or otherwise,

they justified the right of certain nations to conquer, rule and actively transform those 'others' whom they branded as inferior to themselves.

The first questions that many modern historians ask about the records are: who wrote them, and why? With regard to colonial histories, they may want to know: were the subject people passive? What was the response to conquest? Did the subject people collaborate? By what strategies did they resist? Which features of the rulers' culture did they adopt? What of their own culture did they preserve, and by what means?

To answer questions such as these, historians have been helped by other specialists such as archaeologists, linguists and anthropologists.

Early writings on the history of the Cape herders and hunters consisted largely of negative stereotypes: robbers, vagrants, drunkards and a feckless class of servants needing firm control. In 'The Hotnot Syndrome', Smith has shown that such images appear in many textbooks and have become embedded in the pool of information which we share.

How did this happen? If these perceptions are misleading, how may they be changed? The sources include not only written records but pictorial evidence as well. We need to examine these sources and look for grounds for re-interpreting them. The records are rich in personal detail of the Khoikhoi and San. In this book we have included short biographies which enable us to see a range of lifestyles and responses to colonisation.

countries they visited, less damage would have been done. Too often, diplomacy gave way to force when the Khoikhoi or San appeared to block their demands, such as for meat and water.

Further contacts before 1652

For 165 years after da Gama, and before the first white settlement at the Cape, the fleets of European nations called at the few safe anchorages offered by the coast of southern Africa. These mariners, whether agents of monarchs or servants of merchant companies, were concerned with exploration and trade. Where trade prospects appeared good, coastal forts and factories were built and garrisoned. The Portuguese established Elmina in the Gulf of Guinea, Luanda in Angola, Kilwa in East Africa and other settlements where goods such as gold and slaves were available. But the Cape of Good Hope did not attract the Europeans until the Dutch hit upon the idea of refreshing their crews with meat and vegetables at Table Bay.

Nevertheless, much information and comment about the hunters, herders and coastal dwellers described simply as 'scavengers', accumulated during this period. More than 150 voyagers' accounts, of varying length and richness of detail, have been collected together in Raven-Hart's book *Before Van Riebeeck*. Modern scholars know that the various groups living in the south-western Cape had different lifestyles, but for a long time they were all lumped together under labels such as 'natives' or 'blacks'. The fact that the herders called themselves Khoikhoi (or *Kwena*, or *Khoe-na*), while the small foraging groups used names particular to themselves, was only

grasped later on.

Evidence of European cultural contempt for the indigenous people of the south-western Cape becomes more plentiful as time goes on. Their reputation for savagery and bloodthirstiness after the hostilities against de Saldanha (1503) and, more especially, d'Almeida (1510) was enough to persuade the Portuguese to bypass the Cape anchorages whenever they could. For this reason there are almost no written records for the following 60 years, until the English and Dutch fleets began to call. How greatly the Cape dwellers were feared is clear in the first English account in 1579: in spite of urgent need, the English sailors did not go ashore, seeing 'the shore so evill, that nothing could take land, and the land itselfe so full of Tigers, and people that are savage and killers of all strangers'.

In 1605 an English mariner wrote that the region was 'inhabited by a most savage and beastly people as ever I thinke God created'. Here, something more than 'savagery' is implied. The revulsion which fills so many accounts was based on several perceptions of the appearance and habits of the people of the Cape. The earliest observers all believed that they were without religion. This was a severe condemnation in such a deeply religious age. 'They live without law or religion, like animals', it was said in 1610, and this was repeated down the years. 'They have no ceremonies of religion, and do not know what God is', Etienne de Flacourt declared after his visit to the Cape just four years before Van Riebeeck arrived. Another serious charge was that of cannibalism, as we have seen in chapter 1. The rumours ranged from a generalised fear that such heathen must be man-eaters, to the allegation that they dug up buried corpses in order to eat them.

The Khoikhoi were variously described as 'ugly', 'shameless', 'beastly' and 'thievish'; they were written of as puny and ill formed, though many early drawings showed them otherwise; they twined themselves in guts and smeared themselves with animal fat; they stank; they mutilated themselves by cutting off certain fingers at their joints; they ate bloody meat and dirty intestines; they practised infanticide and left their old people in the open to die; the men took several wives; they exposed their 'privies' on request, though these were carelessly covered at the best of times; their language was too crude for speech by those more civilised; and they stole, cheated and were untrustworthy in dealings with the Europeans who came to them in hope of honest trade. As for their 'laziness', it was remarked that they 'devote themselves to idleness, for they neither dig nor spin'. This complaint was heard more often after 1652, when the Dutch settlers required a labour supply. Descriptions such as these, by Europeans who neither questioned nor explained them, made the name 'Hottentot' a synonym for degradation. Our histories and textbooks reflect these perceptions.

Some of the sources of conflict between Europeans and the Cape people have already been shown. Ignoring herder customs with regard to access to water sources was one. Another was the strong protectiveness of the San and Khoikhoi men towards their women, children and encampments. Both the (presumed) hunters at St Helena Bay and the herders at Mossel Bay resisted Por-tuguese attempts to accompany them to their homes. The women and children allowed themselves to be seen only belatedly, keeping their distance. One encounter, in 1510, took a fatal turn because the Portuguese leader was persuaded by his men to take revenge on a Khoikhoi village.

In 1510 the Viceroy of Portuguese India, Francesco de Almeida, was returning to Europe. Events show the arrogance with which the Portuguese regarded the Khoikhoi in Table Bay. As the historian Eric Axelson describes it, an initial friendly meeting and exchange of goods was marred by certain members of the crew seizing one of the Khoikhoi as hostage, so that the others would bring more animals for trade. This backfired on them when the Khoikhoi, 'outraged at this violation of their hospitality', immediately attacked the Portuguese. The situation was made worse when the Portuguese crew members who had attempted to take the hostage, reported to de Almeida that the problem began with the aboriginal herders, who had refused to sell them any livestock. A Portuguese force was sent ashore to teach the Khoikhoi a lesson. They captured several children and drove the cattle to the shore. A large party of the Khoikhoi responded angrily and were able to drive the Portuguese back to their boats, killing a number of them in the process, including de Almeida. The recorder of this incident suggested that 170 'savages' overwhelmed a well-trained force of 150 Portuguese, many from noble families, and he describes how, when they

> were already some way from the village, bringing some cattle, and some children which they had found in the

houses, the blacks ... began to come down from where they had assembled in their first fright, like men who go to risk death to save their sons ... And although some of our folk began to let the children go ... the blacks came on so furiously that they ... came into the body of our men, taking back the oxen; and by whistling to these and making other signs ... they made them surround our men ... like a defensive wall, from behind which came so many fire- hardened sticks that some of us began to fall wounded or trodden by the cattle.

For eighty years after the event, this disastrous image of the Cape kept Europeans away from the land. It was only dispelled when Lancaster, an English captain, landed in Table Bay in 1591 and found what real bargains he could get by trading metals for livestock.

From the very beginning there was an imbalance in the way both sides viewed each other. Several of the Khoikhoi traits which were used to belittle them, such as smearing with grease, or stealing, can be looked at, instructively, from the point of view of modern-day African herdsmen. Among the Himba of Kaokoland in northern Namibia and the Masai of Kenya and Tanzania, fat is mixed with powdered red ochre and rubbed on the body. As Margie Jacobsohn has noted,

Figure 37. European and Khoikhoi traders, with Table Mountain and Table Bay in the background. The two groups of traders are given almost equal status, but the wildness of the Cape is exaggerated: note the snake, the tortoise and the monkey

Coree, the 'Souldania man' (? – c. 1626)

In May 1613 two Khoikhoi were seized by English sailors in Table Bay, which was still called Saldanha, the name given by the Portuguese. They were taken aboard the 300-ton *Hector*, an East Indiaman. The purpose of the abductions seems to have been the same as when in 1554, five West Africans were taken to England in order to learn English and help some English merchants in the West African trade.

Elphick believes that Coree belonged to the leading family of the Gorachouqua, herders who moved around with their cattle in the vicinity of Table Bay. At the time of the Dutch settlement,

60

in 1652, the chief of this group was named Choro, or Chora, which may also have been Coree's correct name. The man abducted with Coree died on the voyage; Coree was taken into the London home of Sir Thomas Smythe, governor of the English East India Company.

Smythe had interests in several chartered companies, used his own fortune to finance voyages of exploration, and at one time served as special emissary to the Russian tsar. He must have regarded Coree's education and exposure to the mercantilist world as important, to have taken him into his own home. Smythe ordered that Coree should receive 'good diet, good cloathes, good lodging', and also 'had ... made for him a chain of bright brass, an armour, breast, back, and head-piece, with a buckler all of brass, his beloved metal'. But Coree was not so easily pleased: 'all this contented him not ... when he had learned a little of our language, he would daily lie upon the ground, and cry very often thus in broken English, "Coree home go. Souldania go, home go."'

In June 1614, Coree was returned to Table Bay. The Europeans noted that the herders at once demanded brass 'of which metle we suppose that Quore, which retorned with us, had geven them knowledg off which was all the kindnes he requited us'. Coree disappeared with his 'tinckerlie treasure', the brass armour and javelin, and, on this occasion, was not seen again. Later it was observed that Coree had 'returned to his old bitts of gutts around his necke', and 'got his sheeps skins upon his back' again.

The way the Europeans described Coree usually depended on the satisfaction they had from him in trade. He was very hospitable to English mariners in 1615, taking them to see his village (around 100 'smale Cottages') and trading 'sheepe and cattell in great aboundance' for copper. By 1617 the mood had changed. The Dutch, it was alleged, had frightened the herders by forcing their way 'into the Contrye', sending large parties of armed men to seize 'soe many Cattell as they will have for nothing'. As a result they complained that 'the *Black* gent *Corre* & his hellish crewe' supplied almost no animals at all. Despite the other reasons given above, traders agreed that Coree, by upsetting the values which the Khoikhoi had attached to European goods, must take the blame for spoiling the trade.

Coree's status within his clan before the English abducted him is not known. On his return, it is 'conceivable', in Elphick's words, 'that his authority among Khoikhoi derived, like that of several later Khoikhoi, from his influence with Europeans'.

Coree died, probably at the hands of the Dutch, in about 1626.

the shine of the red ochre on the body is like the gleam off the back of a beautiful red ox, an observation which suggests the extent to which herders identify with their animals. Taking an item for use is not called stealing among African herdsmen, who mostly hold their possessions in common. Anything that is needed is just taken, and then passed on to anyone else who has need of it. Private possession of property, except domestic animals, is an alien concept to pastoralists.

When applied to land and resources, it explains why people from Europe had difficulty understanding the Khoikhoi. Different clans controlled the grazing and water resources in the western and southern Cape, but no individual within the clan owned any of the land. It was all held in common. This was important as the animals had to be moved around throughout the year to find adequate grazing and water.

Friction arose between Khoi and European out of trade. The records show that both parties were suspicious of being cheated. They show how the Khoikhoi kept the Europeans close to the shore, resisted their attempts to send trading parties inland, and watched for signs that the whites might settle down. One such sign would have been the purchase of more animals than they could reasonably take on board. The Europeans hid their irritation when thefts occurred – usually of metal objects such as shovels and kettles – lest the trade in animals be harmed. They even pretended not to notice when animals they had paid for were stolen and resold:

> And many tymes, havinge sould them
> to us, if we looked not the better to
> them, they would steale them agayne
> from us and bring them agayne to sell;
> which we were fayne with patience to
> buy agayne of them, without givinge
> any foule language, for feare least they
> would bring us noe more.

For many years the Khoikhoi welcomed iron, in the form of bars, strips such as barrel hoops, or nails, in exchange for their sheep and cattle. They used it mainly for assegai heads since metal was superior to horn, or fire-hardened wood tips. But by 1610 the records reveal a growing preference for copper over iron. Elphick, in his book on the early interaction between Khoikhoi and Europeans, states that this happened because the distribution of iron, used for weapons, was controlled by the Table Bay Khoikhoi. On the other hand copper, used for ornamentation, was allowed to be traded freely with rivals inland. What importance we can place on the potential military impact of iron-tipped weapons is not easy to ascertain. Certainly, it would appear that Europeans were wary of the Khoikhoi's fighting skills, while the Khoikhoi appear to have become very eager to trade. Metals may, therefore, have played an increasingly greater social role in Khoikhoi society. The Europeans were annoyed at this rise in demand for copper. Copper was more costly and less plentiful than iron. They were less pleased still when a demand for brass was made, and blamed Coree for this.

In 1647 the Dutch ship *Haerlem* was blown aground in Table Bay. Some of the crew, superintended by the merchant Leendert Janssen, lived on the shore for a full year. After Janssen returned home, he and Matthys Proot, who had also visited the Cape, wrote the Remonstrance. This was a plea addressed to the directors of the Dutch East India Company, the Heren XVII, to establish a fort and place of refreshment in Table Bay. The two men claimed that the indigenous people were manageable and would be useful to such a project. Their Remonstrance refers to the Khoikhoi in terms more favourable than many previous references:

> Others will say that the natives are
> brutish and cannibals, from whom

nothing good is to be expected, and that we shall have to be on our guard continually ... It is not to be denied that they are without laws or government like many Indians, and it is indeed true, that also some sailors and soldiers have been killed by them; but the reason for this is always left unspoken by our folk, to excuse themselves for having been the cause of it, since we firmly believe that the peasants of this country [Holland], if their cattle were to be shot down and taken off without payment, would not show themselves a whit better than these natives, had they not to fear the law.

Janssen and Proot refuted the old charge of cannibalism, and testified to the Khoikhoi's friendliness and openness to fair trade. They stated:

If the proposed fort is provided with a good commander, treating the natives with kindness, and gratefully paying for everything bartered from them, and entertaining some of them with stomachfuls of peas or beans (which they are greatly partial to), then nothing whatever would need to be feared, but in time they would learn the Dutch language, and through them the inhabitants of the Soldania Bay and of the interior might well be brought to trade, of whom however, nothing definite can be said.

The authors believed that if their advice were followed, Khoikhoi children would become available as 'boys and servants', and opportunities would arise to bring 'many souls ... to God, and to the Christian Reformed Religion'.

Jan van Riebeeck, the chosen commander, had no quarrel with the proposed language and evangelisation policies, but he felt that

although Mr Leendert Janz does not appear to entertain much apprehension of any interruption from the natives, provided they are well treated, I say, notwithstanding, that they are by no means to be trusted, but are a savage set, living without conscience, and therefore the Fort should be rendered tolerably defensible, for I have frequently heard, from divers persons equally deserving of credit (who have also been there) that our people have been beaten to death by them, without having given the slightest cause.

The Remonstrance was the framework for the formal instructions to Van Riebeeck regarding policy towards the local people, but he was reminded also of the need for haste in arranging adequate defence against these 'rude people'.

There were sound reasons, both economic and political, for the Dutch to hope that friendly relations with the Table Bay herders might result. But, failing that, European experience of colonisation had taught that, if friendship with natives nearest to their settlements did not work out, deals could be made with those living beyond them, who might see the opportunity in a different light. The most idealistic thinkers of the time felt that force was acceptable where useful projects were blocked by what the colonisers saw as ignorance and indolence. As Sir Thomas More explained in *Utopia* (1516), the Utopians should feel free to expand

wherever the natives have much unoccupied and uncultivated land, [and] found a colony under their own laws. They join with themselves the natives if they are willing to dwell with them ... If they resist, they wage war against them. They consider it a most just cause for war when a people which does not use its soil but keeps it idle and waste nevertheless forbids the use and possession of it to others who by rule of nature ought to be maintained by it.

There may be no direct links between the beliefs of Dutch mercantilists of the 1600s and this English humanist, but they were clearly thinking along the same lines.

We do not know what the Khoikhoi and the San thought about these things. Nevertheless, there is evidence to support some general conclusions as to their ideas. They were often prepared to trade, but would not always agree to a one-sided setting of the rates of exchange. They were able to govern and support themselves, and saw little need to adopt different clothing (although they enjoyed exotic finery), build grander structures, or till the soil.

The Remonstrance recommended teaching some of the Khoikhoi to speak Dutch as an aid to trade, but there was no suggestion of the Dutch learning a Khoikhoi language. Since the Khoikhoi had learned a few words of Dutch from the *Haerlem* experience, they were somewhat preconditioned to deal with the Dutch colonists on the colonists' terms less than five years later. They were prepared to learn a European language, and work for Europeans if they were paid, but they had no natural disposition to become servants on terms which were alien to their economies. In short, they would put up with the presence of outsiders who did not offend their beliefs, destroy their resources, use force against them or – as time would show – settle permanently upon their land.

Khoikhoi, San & Dutch: 1652–1700

6

Within hours of the Dutch landing on the evening of 6 April 1652, they were approached by two groups of people. The first, a small group of men, women and children whom the Dutch called *strandlopers*, were 'only fishers' who kept no livestock. They camped near the new arrivals' tents.

The leader of this group, the Goringhaikonas, was 'Harry', or Autshumato (see box), who spoke some English. The Dutch took him aboard and gave him 'meat and drink'. Autshumato had a long history of contact with European fleets, including a trip (around 1631–2) to Bantam in Java where he was taken by the English for reasons not unlike those which inspired their abduction of Coree. Although the Dutch suspected that he remained loyal to their English rivals, he was 'the Ottentoo who speaks English' and they were friendly towards him for this reason.

The '9 or 10 savages' who appeared next were herders. They may have been Goringhaiquas, the nearest stock-owning group who were not on friendly terms with the Goringhaikonas. A month after the arrival of the Dutch there is mention in Van Riebeeck's *Journal* of fighting between them, resulting in two deaths. It is not clear what the social position of

Figure 38. This painting of the Dutch landing in 1652, called 'Jan van Riebeeck meets the Hottentots', shows the Commander flanked by a merchant, a minister of the Reformed Church, and soldiers. By various techniques the artist contrasts the Dutch with the indigenous inhabitants. The picture was painted by C.D. Bell in 1850 to celebrate the Van Riebeeck bicentenary in 1852.

the Goringhaikonas was. It is probable that they were stockless, therefore low-status, Khoikhoi. Later they stole Dutch cattle and knew how to take care of the stock.

The members of the second group were 'very handsome active men, of particularly good stature, dressed however in a cow (or ox) hide tolerably prepared, which they carried gracefully upon one arm, with an air as courageous as any bravo in Holland can carry his cloak on arm or shoulder.' They promised to come back with sheep and cattle, in which the Dutch 'encouraged them by good and

liberal treatment'. But except for a lean cow and calf (for which they got copper), they disappointed the Dutch for many months. It took the settlers time to understand that seasonal grazing contributed to this, apart from the herders' reluctance to trade away their stock.

Van Riebeeck acted promptly to erect a fort and regulate relations with the 'natives'. He issued the first of many edicts to prohibit private barter: all trade should be conducted on the Dutch East India Company's behalf.

The colonists had to live off fresh fish until 19 October when the first of the

Figure 39. Van Riebeeck met Khoikhoi who were dressed, as this man is, with a cow-hide cloak draped over one arm. Note also the ivory arm-ring which was not just ornamental, but was used to ward off kierie blows when fighting. Artist unknown, early 1700s, SA Library.

Goringhaiqua brought animals for trade. This was because the local herdsmen did not pasture their animals at the coast during winter – early evidence of the seasonal round of the Khoikhoi. The pattern is different from that experienced by the previous European visitors to Saldanha Bay. There it was only during winter that the sailors had any chance of meeting the Khoikhoi at the coast with animals. In summer no trade was possible since the herds were all inland.

These seemingly contradictory observations are easily explained. The Cape Peninsula has some rain in summer, so there is year-round pasture available. By using the coastal resources between October and January they would leave the interior pastures to regenerate until the winter. At Saldanha Bay, the rainfall drops off markedly before midsummer, and the summer pastures are inadequate for free-ranging cattle herds. In that area the Khoikhoi would only come to the coast in winter, after the rains.

The next piece of information about the Khoikhoi from the daily journal kept

Autshumato, called 'Harry': *strandloper* chief and Van Riebeeck's first interpreter (c. 1611 – 1663)

It is not clear when the Europeans first met *strandlopers*, or 'Watermen', at Table Bay. Hunters and herders had exploited marine resources at many points along the coast of southern Africa over a long period of time, but the small group of 50 or so at Table Bay was unusual in that it was made up of hunters, cattleless herders and outcasts of various kinds. This band may have formed as a response to the peculiar opportunities which arose from the visits of ships from Europe. Its leading men received small gifts in return for serving as postmasters, supplying intelligence about the hinterland and rival fleets, assisting with the 'refreshing' of ships, and acting as intermediaries when herders happened to appear.

Autshumato became the most important of these men. After his return from Bantam, where he was taken in an English merchantman (c. 1631–2), he acted as agent for the English and, on occasion, for the Dutch.

When the Van Riebeeck party arrived,

Autshumato was 'acknowledged as the chief of this little tribe' and was employed as broker in the hoped-for livestock trade. The fact that he was a pastoralist, concerned not only to acquire livestock for the Dutch but also for himself, was soon revealed. In October 1653 Autshumato and his followers deserted with the Company's animals, having murdered the Dutch herdboy. But Van Riebeeck needed 'Harry's' chiefly control and his skill as broker and interpreter, and so he reinstated him in 1655.

Soon many Khoikhoi learned to speak Dutch. As far as can be ascertained, Autshumato spoke only English. At the same time, Van Riebeeck realised that there were many Khoikhoi groups, and that these groups were often hostile to one another. Trusting none, Van Riebeeck employed several interpreters at once and played them off against each other to the Company's advantage – or

so he hoped. At first Autshumato flourished in this scheme. As his wealth in livestock increased, so his influence was seen to extend beyond his *strandlopers* to include local herders. But in July 1658 his fortunes were reversed. In the course of trying to force the Khoikhoi to recover some escaped slaves, Van Riebeeck took Autshumato hostage and confiscated his stock. He was imprisoned first at the Dutch fort and then on Robben Island, a place he had known from pre-colonial days.

In December 1659, Autshumato escaped from Robben Island in a leaky boat and landed near Bloubergstrand. Although he was once more reinstated at the Fort, and even earned occasional praise, 'Harry' was little better than 'a beggar' from then on. The Dutch gave other Khoikhoi the chance to become 'thriving merchants' in the Company's employ. Autshumato died in 1663, a year after Van Riebeeck left the Cape.

by the Fort is that no matter how eager the Khoikhoi were for metal, they were reluctant to give up their stock, particularly their breeding cows. As the *Journal* notes on 5 November 1654: 'These rogues are not at all keen to part with their cattle and sheep, although they have an abundance of fine stock.'

Each Khoikhoi group had its own territory. This is clear from the descriptions found in the *Journal*, and in reports from sailors and shipwrecked travellers. There were two stock-owning groups who used the pastures between the Hottentots Holland Mountains and the Cape Peninsula. These were the Goringhaiqua and the Gorachoqua or 'Peninsulars', whose territory probably extended as far north

as Malmesbury (fig. 40).

To the north of this was the land of the Cochoqua, which included Saldanha Bay and the Vredenberg Peninsula, across to the mountains at Porterville. The Chariguriqua appear to have occupied the lower Berg River area and points around the Piketberg. The entire coastal forelands of the south-western Cape were quite densely occupied by pastoralists. Up the west coast the Klein Namaqua used the pastures of Namaqualand beyond today's Van Rhynsdorp as far as the Orange River or Gariep. North of the Orange was the land of the Groot Namaqua. Along the Orange River, between the Augrabies Falls and present-day Upington, were the Einiqua, and upriver of them were the Korana. About where Upington is today there was a mixed Khoikhoi–BaThlaping (Tswana) group called Geziqua. These people were probably intermediaries who assisted in the trade between the Khoikhoi and BaThlaping (called Blip or Bliquas by early observers). Wikar describes the trade in 1779: 'The Blip came each year to the tribes living along this river to trade, bringing with them tobacco, ivory spoons, bracelets, copper and iron beads, glass beads, copper earrings and bracelets, knives, barbed assegais and also smooth axes and awls.'

Along the south coast the forelands were occupied by various Khoikhoi groups. Just over the Hottentots Holland Mountains on the Caledon plains were the Chainoqua, a large and powerful group who later brought stock to trade with the colony. To the east of the Chainoqua were the Hessequa, and in the region of Mossel Bay lived the Gouriqua,

possibly the same people met by Bartolomeu Dias. The Houteniqua/Attaqua were to be found in the region between George and Plettenberg Bay, and were probably the people who traded with the survivors of the wreck of the *São Gonçalo* in 1630, as the historian Eric Axelson has suggested. Beyond was the country of the Gamtoos, who lived in the Algoa Bay area and who made contact with the survivors of the wrecked *Nossa Senhora de Atalaia* in 1647.

One of the early expeditions sent out from the colony at Table Bay in 1689 was that of Isaq Schrijver. His instructions were to make contact with a group of Khoikhoi called the Inqua. Schrijver and his men passed through the country of the Hessequas and Attaquas (fig. 40).

Figure 40. Approximate locations of Khoikhoi before contact with whites (in the south-western Cape c. 1650; in the south-eastern Cape and along the Orange River c. 1750). After Elphick, 1977.

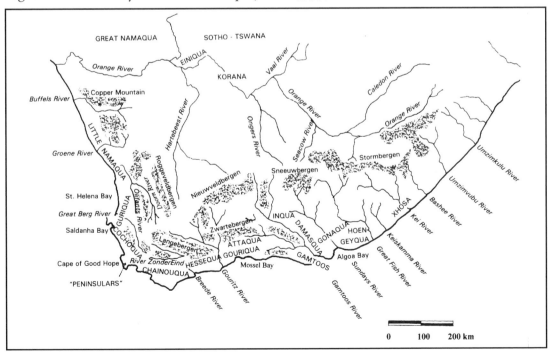

The expedition had to rely on the guidance of some Sonqua to take them to chief Heijkon, leader of the Inqua, whom they met on Saturday, 19 February 1689. He is described as being 'of great stature and more robust than any of our men'. From these people the Dutch were able to barter for over 500 cattle. They also learned of the people to the east who lived in clay houses. These included the Gonaqua, a mixed Khoikhoi–Xhosa group, as well as the Xhosa themselves. From their informants the Dutch learned of the trade in copper and dagga between the black African farmers and the Khoikhoi. Relations between the Inqua and the Sonqua were strained, as the herders were very aware of the possibility of a raid by the hunters.

So far as the records reveal, Van Riebeeck's first contact with hunter–gatherers occurred in 1655 when J. Wintervogel's expedition came upon 'a certain people of very small stature, subsisting very meagrely, quite wild, without huts, cattle or anything in the world, clad in small skins like these Hottentots and speaking almost as they do.'

At first the Dutch used the Khoikhoi names for these cattleless inhabitants of the interior, calling them Sonqua or Ubiqua. But they soon made up their own name for them: in 1682 the expedition leader Ensign Olof Bergh wrote of meeting 'Somquaas, alias Bushmen' and in 1685 the *Journal* of Governor Simon van der Stel refers to 'Sonquas, commonly called Bosjesmans'. Though they could not always understand the relationship between the hunters and herders, the Dutch recorded some of the differences they noticed. According to Van der Stel: 'These Sonquas are just the same as the

poor in Europe, each tribe of Hottentots having some of them and employing them to bring news of the approach of a strange tribe.' Elsewhere he states: '[The Ubiqua] maintain themselves by robbing and stealing from other Hottentots, having no cattle at all nor anything else on which to live.'

The first contacts between Dutch and San were friendly, but in 1669 some eastern Ubiqua rained poisoned arrows on an expedition led by Hieronimus Cruse. This aggression may have been provoked by the presence in Cruse's party of certain Khoikhoi, including Dorha, an up-and-coming ally of the Dutch (see p. 78). The indigenous societies were changing under the impact of colonisation. Some herders, such as Dorha, believed that their best chance of survival lay in allying themselves with the Dutch; others who had lost their livestock had to live as hunters, like the Ubiqua. Out of concern for their own safety and commercial prospects, the Dutch closely observed the hunters and herders. Sometimes, however, they did not fully understand the changes which were taking place.

The First Khoikhoi–Dutch War
The herders soon became aware of the full implications of the Dutch presence. Because so many fleets had come and gone, and even the stranded *Haerlem* crew had finally sailed away, it seems the Khoikhoi first believed that the Van Riebeeck party would not stay. By 1656 their eyes were open. When the Dutch ordered Autshumato and others to remove their stock from pastures near the Fort, 'Harry maintained that the land of the Cape belonged to him and the Kaapmans [Goringhaiqua], but he was

told that [as] the Company also required pasturage ... his claim to ownership of this Cape could not be entertained'. A year later when the first freeburgher farms were given out, Autshumato was told that, to retain any claim to local pasturage, the herders must satisfy the Dutch demand for barter stock. This was as unacceptable to Khoikhoi pastoralists as was the sight of prime pastures disappearing under the burghers' ploughs.

There was, understandably, considerable frustration on the part of the colonists when they realised that the Khoikhoi were reluctant to trade their stock. This was one reason for spreading the contact to other Khoikhoi groups further afield, in the hope that they would be more willing to give up part of their herds. There was a complete misunderstanding by the Dutch of the value of cattle to the Khoikhoi, as well as how nomadic pastoralists lived. The Dutch, as all Europeans, were used to land being owned by individuals. Land was a commodity which could be exchanged or sold. Similarly, stock was merely a commodity in the Dutch mind, and had monetary, but not symbolic, value.

In 1659 the newly-formed burgher

Doman: pastoralist, interpreter and military strategist (d. December 1663)

In 1655 Autshumato persuaded the Dutch to sponsor him so he could buy livestock on the Company's behalf. While he was absent from the fort, two new interpreters were employed. The first, who was a Waterman and Autshumato's choice, was Khaik Ana Ma Koukoa, called Claes Das by the Dutch. The second was Doman. There are two ideas about Doman's name. The first is that it is from *dominee*, or parson. But Elphick suggests a Khoikhoi root, '*domi-*' meaning 'voice', based on the fact that he was able to translate their language into Dutch. Of this man Van Riebeeck's diarist wrote:

> We called aside a certain other Hottentot calling himself Doman or Domine – a name by which we also now call him because he is such an artless person – who seems to be well-disposed towards us and, together with the Hottentot Claes Das, has been employed in Harry's place as interpreter. As such he is serving the Hon. Company better than anybody else – up to the present at any rate.

Distrust of interpreters, if not of Khoikhoi in general, can be seen in this extract. In spite of this, the Dutch cannot have learned from past experience the dangers of exposing selected Khoikhoi to foreign places. In April 1657 Commissioner R. van Goens, charged with advising Van Riebeeck regarding defence and other matters at the Cape, took Doman to Java, from where he returned in 1658.

While Doman was away, Krotoa who had been reared by the Van Riebeecks in the Fort, had made herself useful as interpreter. After Doman's return the two often clashed – partly because they spoke for rival groups. At one point, Krotoa claimed that Doman said: 'I am a Hottentot and not a Dutchman, but you, Eva, try to curry favour with the Commander.'

With their own ears the Dutch heard Doman's jibe, 'See, there comes the advocate of the Dutch; she will tell her people some stories and lies and will finally betray them all.'

After Autshumato's banishment, Krotoa took over as the main manager of barter at the fort. When the cattle-rich Cochoqua brought some livestock in May 1659, they publicly 'thrashed' Doman when he tried to intervene. He next appeared amongst a 'robber' band.

Though not an hereditary chief, or a man of outstanding wealth, Doman had a following and, it had been noted, behaved 'like a master, in Harry's manner'. He came strongly to the fore in the First Khoikhoi–Dutch War (1659–60) when the herders attempted to expel the colonists. He offered firm political convictions – the Khoikhoi must eject the Dutch, or else submit to them as had the Javanese. He also offered knowledge of the weaknesses of the Dutch in combat.

He led attacks on rainy days when the powder of Dutch muskets would not ignite and won several victories. But on 19 July 1659, a musketball severely injured Doman, paralysing an arm. Although he survived, he sought refuge at Saldanha Bay and the war, for this and other reasons, petered out.

Doman, like Autshumato, was allowed to return to the fort after peace treaties with the Goringhaiqua and Gorachouqua were arranged (April and May 1660). On 11 December 1663, Doman died. The entry in Governor Wagenaer's journal reads: 'This evening died, in a Hottentoo's hut outside of the Fort, the Company's interpreter Doman; for whose death none of us will have cause to grieve, as he has been, in many respects, a mischievous and malicious man towards the Company.'

militia was called out, when the Khoikhoi captured seven of the Company's draught oxen. It was later explained that the herders 'had begun the war against us because we had put all the best ground under the plough and they had thought they would be able to prevent this by stealing the oxen we used for ploughing'. In this, the first Khoikhoi–Dutch war, a new-style Khoikhoi leader played a prominent part, as the box about Doman reveals.

At the talks which ended the war, the Khoikhoi objected in the strongest terms to the thefts and cruelties of the burghers and the taking of their land, asking 'who should rather in justice give way, the rightful owner or the foreign intruder?' However, the Dutch defended their right to keep what they had 'won by the sword'.

Khoikhoi in the early colonial records

For the first twenty years of Dutch settlement (1652–72), the most important records for the historian are: the journals and despatches of the Cape commanders (who were given the status of governor in 1671); the resolutions and proclamations (*plakkaaten*) of the Council of Policy, the ruling body at the Cape; the memoranda and instructions received from the Governor–General in Batavia, the Heren XVII (directors of the Dutch East India Company, which was privately owned), and the commissioners appointed by the Company to address specific issues; and accounts by callers at the Cape – those travellers who visited and then sailed on.

Before the 1670s, the Khoikhoi were treated as independent people under the governance of their chiefs. Throughout its trading empire, the Company favoured indirect rule, that is, leaving local chiefs in place so long as they obeyed the Dutch. However, an incident in 1671 resulted in an acknowledgement that some Khoikhoi should be subject to the colonial court. Soon after this, five independent herders who assaulted and stole from colonists were sentenced by the Council of Justice at the Fort to floggings and imprisonment. From this point the records of the Court of Justice are also sources of information about the Khoikhoi.

On 1 May 1659, Van Riebeeck established a freeburgher militia to combat livestock thefts. This resulted in many reports by *veldkorporaals* (burgher officers) and the *Krygsraad* (council of war). In the late 1600s new centres of government were created at Stellenbosch and Drakenstein (Paarl). Notes on the meetings of Landdrosts and Heemraden (the local officials) in the hinterland became an important source of information about the San and Khoikhoi.

Although all these documents reflect the objectives and practices of the colonists, they also shed light on the goals and strategies of the indigenous people. The colonists desired security for themselves and unhindered trade for meat and other goods. They needed labourers to produce food, to relieve Company servants of tasks such as fetching water and wood, and to build the fort, hospital and other fixtures. To these ends, Company officials wooed the herders with gifts, especially of drink and food, and protected them as best they could from the greed of Europeans whose only interest was benefiting themselves.

The Dutch governors found that 'well-treated' herders still would not barter

Figure 41. The Dutch settlement at the Cape wooed the Khoikhoi with gifts of drink and food. Here, a Khoikhoi man is given a drink by a colonist, receiving it in his kaross. Unknown artist, early 1700s, SA Library.

livestock freely, give up their pasture-lands, or exchange their traditional pastoralism for a life as wage labourers. Thus we find reprisals in the form of hostage-taking and banishment; the making and breaking of alliances; the strengthening of defensive systems; periodic wars; allocation of herders' land to freeburghers; secret scheming to enslave Khoikhoi; and bans to keep arms and ammunition out of Khoikhoi hands.

Christianity

The authors of the Remonstrance (see p. 62) had foreseen the winning of 'many souls ... to God, and to the Christian Reformed religion', should the Company establish a station at the Cape. But baptism into the Reformed Protestant church was as much a political as a theological issue in colonies where the bulk of the population was 'heathen'.

Heads of households at the Cape were responsible for instructing in the Christian religion all those, including the hea-

Krotoa, called 'Eva': interpreter and first Khoikhoi Christian convert (c. 1642–1674)

Krotoa, who was about ten years old in 1652, was living among the *strandlopers* at the time of the founding of the Dutch settlement. Autshumato was always described as her uncle, while her mother was thought to live among the Goringhaiqua. (Because of the differences in Khoikhoi and European kinship systems, caution must be used with regard to these alleged relationships.) Later she was found to have important connections among other herding groups.

In his memorandum to his successor (1662), Van Riebeeck stated that the *strandlopers*, or Goringhaikona, often placed 'their little daughters in the service of the married people' among the colonists. A *Journal* entry in October 1657 described 'Eva' as having been 'in the service of the Commander's wife from the beginning'.

Krotoa learned to speak Dutch as perfectly as any Dutch girl, and also to speak Portuguese. When at the Fort she wore 'clothing' and was said to like the 'Dutch diet'. After a stage where it seemed she might permanently rejoin her Khoikhoi family, and perhaps marry an important chief, she returned to the fort and professed a deepened interest in Christianity. However lax others of the settlers may have been in teaching their religion to 'heathen' servants, the Van Riebeecks managed to produce a convert. Krotoa was baptised as 'Eva', the name by which she was always known to the Dutch.

Krotoa was never really trusted by the Dutch. Nor did she retain the trust of the Khoikhoi, to whom she returned from time to time, adopting their customs and dress. It was impossible to satisfy the trading interests of both rivals at once. Doman and Autshumato were angry with her when she told a hopeful Van Riebeeck that the fabled land of Monomotapa lay within reach to the north. Krotoa and Doman were divided on many issues, but she and Autshumato remained close. When he was banished to Robben Island she endured a terrifying trip in a small boat in order to visit him and never ceased to plead for his release, 'begging for her uncle as

74

Esther did for Mordecai'.

After war broke out between the Khoikhoi and the Dutch, Krotoa found herself to be the only Khoikhoi at the fort. When the alliance which Van Riebeeck sought with the Cochoqua did not come about, she experienced the first serious breach in her relationship with the Dutch.

In 1659 the Danish soldier and surgeon, Pieter van Meerhoff, arrived at the Cape. He took part in six Company-sponsored expeditions and proved himself a brave and resourceful man. On 2 June 1664, Krotoa and Van Meerhoff were married and a 'little wedding feast' was given in their honour in the fort. Commander Wagenaer hoped that, as a result, 'these native tribes will become more and more attached to us'.

In fact, Wagenaer had a low opinion of 'Eva': Van Riebeeck had told him how useful she could be but, in the same breath, had warned him of the dual role she sometimes played. She had two children 'won by a European', by 1663. Almost certainly they were van Meerhoff's, but general opinion ever since has been that Krotoa was of low morals. Wagenaer's diarist calls her 'a lewd vixen' at this point.

A year after the wedding, Van Meerhoff was appointed superintendent of Robben Island. This was well known as a lonely post for a superintendent's wife. While there, Krotoa suffered an accident for which drunkenness is usually blamed. In 1667 Van Meerhoff was sent on a voyage to the east African coast; Krotoa and their children waited on Robben Island until, after eight months, the news came that he was 'killed by blacks' at Antongil Bay in Madagascar.

For the remainder of her life, Krotoa was shuttled back and forth between the island and the mainland. Her skills were no longer treated as of any use and she was regularly described as a prostitute and drunk. At last, when she was said to have abandoned her children, she was arrested and sent as a prisoner to the island. Those who claimed to have witnessed her 'adulterous and debauched life' believed that the care given her in the past was ineffectual in the face of her 'Hottentoo nature'.

Krotoa died on 29 July 1674 and 'notwithstanding her unchristian life' was given a Christian burial inside the Castle which replaced the old Fort. Her children received Christian baptisms and, after a spell in Mauritius, a daughter married a freeburgher and returned with her family to the Cape.

then, assembled under their roofs. A few individuals exerted themselves: Van Riebeeck's brother-in-law, Pieter van der Stael, who came as 'sick-comforter' and teacher to the Cape, tried to bring religion to the *strandlopers* but with poor results. He blamed this on their 'degeneracy', 'infatuation' with cattle, and 'ignorance' of the existence of God. Pierre Simond, a Huguenot clergyman who arrived in 1688, was initially keen to civilise (*prendre d'humaniser*) two or three bands near Stellenbosch. This, he informed the Heren XVII, would bring glory to the Company. The intention clearly was to Europeanise (*faire habiller comme nous*) the Khoikhoi.

On the political side, being a Christian was linked with burghership. Christians did not automatically become burghers,

Fig. 1. pag. 470. Tab. P. zu pag. 470. Tab. XIV.

Wie die Hottentotten ihr Rind Vieh und die Schafe zu Nachts benahren.

Figure 42. How the Khoikhoi protected their sheep and cattle at night. In the early 1700s it was still possible to see the Khoikhoi living according to their traditions. Peter Kolb, in whose book this engraving appears, left the Cape just before the smallpox epidemic which caused many Khoikhoi deaths in 1713.

but burgher status and the civil rights attached were usually unattainable to those not baptised in the Reformed Protestant church. Most historians would agree that the attitudes which denied baptism to slaves at the Cape 'became a general attitude, as well, toward household and farm servants' drawn from the people of the Cape. There is, in fact, just one known example of Khoikhoi baptism at the Cape in the 1600s. In 1662, before the Van Riebeecks left, Krotoa (Eva) was baptised in the Fort.

Khoikhoi traders

In the search for ideal trading partners, the Company offered hospitality to herders who visited the Fort, sponsored expeditions to the interior, and engaged Khoikhoi to act as brokers and interpreters. When the herders nearest to Table Bay became impoverished or alienated by the difficulties of peaceful coexistence with the Dutch, the opportunities for trade were greatly reduced. More distant herders were drawn into the Company's trading network during the 1660s and 1670s as a result of bartering expedities led by officers such as Olof Bergh and Hieronimus Cruse. In 1689 Ensign Isaq Schrijver brought back many cattle and much information from his three-month journey to the Inqua in the east.

The last important Khoikhoi broker was Dorha, whom the Dutch called Klaas. Dorha was recruited from the Chainouqua, a wealthy group of eastern herders with whom trading relations were maintained for several decades after Van Riebeeck won their friendship with Krotoa's help.

The 1670s, when Dorha came to the fore, were watershed years for the Khoikhoi of the south-western Cape. In 1672 the Dutch concluded two treaties in terms of which the Goringhaiqua and Gorachouqua surrendered considerable tracts of land, from Table Bay to Saldanha Bay in the north and the Hottentots Holland to the east. The compensation actually paid for these concessions was a mere fraction of that promised in treaty documents. Unwittingly perhaps, they also agreed to permit the Company to involve itself in their domestic affairs and to render annual tribute in stock.

In this year, also, certain offences involving Khoikhoi were dealt with under Dutch law. A crime charged to some Cochoqua led to this step. In July 1673 the Council of Policy sent a party under Ensign Cruse to punish the Cochoqua. This was the start of the Second Khoikhoi–Dutch War. The result was total victory for the Dutch. In due course Gonnema, the Cochoqua chief, accepted the Company's staff of office – a brass-headed stick which gave the status of subordinate ally to compliant chiefs.

By 1700, proclamations regulated almost every aspect of herder–settler relations. Those covering the livestock trade were constantly extended and renewed. When it was found that Khoikhoi were using money to buy tobacco, which they used to barter livestock on their own account, the Council of Policy forbade Company servants or freeburghers to pay them in currency. Other restrictions on the Khoikhoi concerned the boarding of ships, transactions involving meat, fruit, tobacco, wood, stolen goods and strong drink, the supply of arms and ammunition, and fraternising with freeburghers in their homes. In 1678 the Council of Policy forbade concubinage with *onchristen vrouwen* – illegal in any case under the Statutes of India, which were meant to be applied in all Dutch possessions.

Of great importance to the herders were actions concerning land: the allocations to the first freeburghers (1657), and the marking out of farms in Stellenbosch (1679) and Paarl (1687). Crucial labour policies include the early employment of *strandlopers* at the Fort, the importation of slaves, and the beginnings of Khoikhoi labour on freeburgher farms. Militarily, some Khoikhoi had been treated as allies, employed side by side with Company soldiers and the burgher militia. At the same time, their leaders had been obliged to accept staffs of office which signified submission to the Company as well as friendship.

Elphick and Giliomee believe that the social hierarchy which evolved at the Cape began with the Company-imposed 'legal status groups', namely: Company servants, freeburghers, slaves and independent 'Hottentots', each with its own

Dorha, called 'Klaas': Chainouqua captain and live-stock broker for the Dutch (c. 1640–1701)

With the death of the respected Chainouqua chief Soeswa in 1663, there seems to have been no heir or other leader of his stature to assume control. Power was divided among lesser men. Though Khoikhoi groups often broke up, when it happened in this case it probably reduced their capacity to resist encroachment by the colonists.

Dorha first appears in the records (as 'Klaas') in 1669 when he went with Ensign Cruse to barter livestock from the Hessequa, friendly neighbours of the Chainouqua who seem to have been even wealthier and more numerous. Cruse reported that 'Klaas' was delighted by the fact that Dutch guns killed some Ubiqua and put the rest to flight. In 1672 he persuaded the Dutch to supply him with trade goods so that he could gain access to the large herds and flocks of eastern Khoikhoi on their behalf. Dorha became a frequent visitor at the old Fort and then the new Castle (completed in 1776). It appears that he complied with all their requests: for information, for guides, for draught animals and for the capture of escaped slaves.

When the Second Khoikhoi–Dutch War (1673–7) broke out, Dorha, along with the other Chainouqua captains, became an ally of the Dutch. The alliance came naturally as the Company wanted to crush the Cochoqua, who were long-standing enemies of the Chainouqua. In 1674 Dorha contributed 250 fighting men to the second expedition which the Company launched against the Cochoqua. Aside from the opportunity to vanquish a rival, participation meant booty in cattle and sheep. The Dutch, who controlled the distribution of booty, gave Dorha some oxen and 300 sheep. Typically the Dutch gave sheep to their Khoikhoi allies, keeping the more highly prized cattle for themselves and those burghers who had taken part.

For twenty years the bargain between Dorha and the Dutch worked to the advantage of each. The Company received more livestock with less trouble and cost than in the past. Dorha acquired extensive herds and flocks. After 1677 there was relative peace: Dorha was on good terms with his powerful neighbour, Chief Gaukou of the Hessequa, whose daughter he married. But in time his wealth made him the special target of thefts, while his political status earned rival leaders' envy and wrath. In 1693, Governor Van der Stel attacked and arrested Dorha on the strength of his rivals' allegations.

It took two years for the Heren XVII to react, but, when convinced that the attack was unjustified, they censured Van der Stel and ordered Dorha's reinstatement. But the damage had already been done. Dorha had lost his influence and his livestock, and also his wife, who had gone over to his rival, Koopman. In June 1701 Dorha was killed, perhaps murdered, at Koopman's place. His years of faithful service to the Dutch were not enough to safeguard his relationship with them, while his leadership among the Khoikhoi was smashed by the scheming of determined enemies.

set of rights, or absence of rights. Recognition of the Khoikhoi as 'free' was upheld and proclamations prohibiting 'mistreatment' were published from time to time. Nevertheless, there are many signs that the lifestyles which had sustained their independence and identities were being undermined. The historical record leads researchers to believe that resistance to settler expansion increased during the next hundred years.

Figure 43. In 1672, just twenty years after the arrival of Van Riebeeck, certain representatives of the Khoikhoi entered into two treaties with the Dutch. In Richard Elphick's words, these treaties 'were written for the benefit of European powers and were obviously not fully explained to the Khoikhoi signatories'. The Khoikhoi received only a fraction of the payments that were first proposed, and in return they gave up control not only of extensive lands, but also of aspects of self-rule.

Khoikhoi, San & colonists in the 1700s

7

For some time it appeared that the records for the 1700s might not give the same amount of information for a history of the Khoikhoi, compared with what was known about the earlier and later periods. In the 1600s the Khoikhoi and, to a lesser extent, the San had been a focus of interest in governors' journals and in dispatches sent between governors and the Company. In the 1800s the Khoikhoi and San were to become the special concern of missionaries who, for a time, helped to make them an important part of records and documents once again. In the 1700s two new districts, Swellendam and Graaff-Reinet, were proclaimed, ensuring the accumulation of documents. But the early archives of Swellendam, established as an independent magistracy in 1745, are very incomplete, partly owing to a disastrous fire. The district of Graaff-Reinet came into being much later, in 1786.

Many of the surviving documents of this period are difficult to read because of the archaic Dutch, fading ink and closely written scrawls. However, the task of re-examining these records has been taken on in recent years and the research has revealed important new information. In addition, historians have taken a fresh look at the writings of offi-

Figure 44. By the early 1700s the Europeans had filled in the map of southern Africa with some names of the indigenous people, but this map is still largely fanciful.

cial explorers and unofficial travellers. It is now possible to describe, more accurately than before, the experiences of hunters and herders in the 1700s.

By 1700 the need of the Dutch settlement at the Cape – and of passing fleets – for food, especially meat, had already made an impact on the neighbouring herders. During the 1700s southern Africa, up to and even beyond the Orange and Fish rivers, was changed by the interaction of colonist and colonised. Eurocentric histories of this period have focused largely on such issues as the quarrels between freeburghers and the Company, the struggle to assert govern-

mental controls in the areas inhabited by trekboer pioneers, and the problems faced by European producers in need of labour. In some of these accounts, the hunters and herders were scarcely mentioned. It was assumed that they had been easily vanquished, were not very good servants and had, in any case, been almost wiped out by disease. But when historians began to inquire more closely into the behaviour of the hunters and herders, they discovered a wealth of information which earlier researchers, whose eyes were fixed on other questions, had failed to notice.

Conflict and resistance in the 1700s

An early instance of Khoikhoi resistance occurred after Governor W. A. van der Stel granted licences to freeburghers to pasture their stock in the Tulbagh basin (then called the Land of Waveren). This move was the result of an order from the Heren XVII to the effect that the Company must stop crop and pastoral farming and give this task to the growing numbers of freemen at the Cape. The policy forbidding burghers to barter with Khoikhoi was reversed, the livestock trade was opened up, and the burghers were instructed to deliver cattle to the Company. These new policies posed serious threats to Khoikhoi control over their pastures, water and wealth in stock.

In 1701 the Dutch on the frontiers were attacked at many points, but most severely in the Land of Waveren. The

Figure 45. Dutch freeburghers who became pastoralists learned much from the Cape herders. Here a farmer and a Khoikhoi man prepare draught oxen for yoking to a wagon. Artist unknown, early 1700s, SA Library.

Figure 46. A farmer armed with a musket sees that lions have attacked one of his herd, and a Khoikhoi family confront a lion with a kierie and a spear. Artist unknown, early 1700s, SA Library.

fact that they called their attackers 'Bosjesmen' misled early historians: there is convincing evidence that the Guriqua, Namaqua and other herders led the attacks (which aimed chiefly at capturing livestock) although hunters were probably involved as well.

It was now common to find some Khoikhoi on the colonists' side in any conflict between the two groups. Some independent herders sought the protection of Dutch guns for their herds and flocks against hunter–robbers and traditional rivals; others worked for freeburghers who let them graze a few animals on their farms. They, too, had welcomed the opportunity to expand into the Tulbagh basin, and they also lost stock in the wave of thefts in the years 1701–3. Although they co-operated with the Dutch after the attacks, and helped them to retrieve stolen animals, the Khoikhoi, as junior partners, were less assured of regaining their former wealth.

In 1702, after the long-standing ban on private barter had been repealed, colonists and Khoikhoi in equal numbers – around 45 of each – went on a journey to the vicinity of modern Somerset East. There they attacked some Xhosa before turning back and raiding large numbers of stock from the richest surviving herder group, the Inqua. They took some 2 000 cattle and 2 500 sheep. In the division of this loot, the Europeans kept most of it for themselves, each Khoikhoi participant receiving a single cow and a few sheep.

The Company's new policy had aimed at increasing food production for the benefit of the Cape settlement and passing ships. On receiving news of this raid, by which a few self-seeking colonists were enriched, the Company reimposed the ban on private barter. But in 1704 it

Figure 47. This drawing from the early 1700s shows 'Hottentot Hutts' where central Cape Town is today.

was again revoked. Meanwhile, in 1703, the Company had begun issuing grazing permits to farmers who applied to take their livestock beyond the settled regions for a period of months. This was the start of the 'loan farm' system, which made the expansion of the trekboers into the interior much easier. From 1713 fees (*recognitiegeld*) had to be paid, but this did little to slow down the trekboers' acquisition of these 2 420 hectare claims. This cost the Khoikhoi and San their choicest pastures and hunting grounds.

Important decisions concerning labour were also taken at this time. The ending of free passages for European immigrants in 1707 may have slowed the rate of land appropriation by white colonists. On the other hand, this decision, together with another in 1717 which supported slave labour over white immigration, affected the way in which labour relations developed at the Cape. Coincidentally, the first known complaint by a Khoikhoi that a colonist had withheld the wages they had agreed upon, took place in 1717. This information comes from Nigel Penn, a historian who has spent many years deciphering the records of the 1700s. Before the 1800s, most contracts were verbal, so we have few records of the bargains that were struck, but the fact that Khoikhoi complaints increased in number during the 1700s supports the impression that labour relations at the Cape were becoming more strained.

Disruption of the indigenous communities in region after region is well documented. Many reasons are given. In

Figure 48. The indigenous people of the western Cape were not crop farmers themselves, but soon learned to carry out essential tasks on the grain farms of the colonists. They built traditional matjieshuise *on the freeburgher farms where they could live in family groups. Here a Khoikhoi asks a passing colonist for some tobacco, while others are seen working or resting. Artist unknown, early 1700s, SA Library.*

1705 the landdrost of Stellenbosch stated that, north of Cape Town, most of the herders who 'used to live contentedly under chiefs, peacefully supporting themselves by breeding cattle' had become 'Bushmen, hunters and robbers, and are scattered everywhere among the mountains'. He blamed this on the greed of the burghers, but this could be due in part to his 'strong bias against freemen', in Elphick's view. After all, the Company itself had done much to reduce the livestock holdings of the Khoikhoi. In 1712 the landdrost, Slotsboo, remarked on the large number of destructive inter-Khoikhoi feuds, at the same time confirming the widespread (though not universal) poverty of herders to the north.

In the following year, 1713, the smallpox epidemic occurred. This has been held up as the main cause of the virtual disappearance of the Khoikhoi from the south-western Cape, and of the deaths of great numbers of indigenous people further inland. The dreadful effect of the epidemic is not in dispute, but there is some debate about the reasons for its severity and the long-term results of the epidemic. As several researchers have pointed out, this disaster was made worse by a drought and by other epidemics which reduced the herds and flocks of Khoikhoi, Company and colonists.

Increasingly, officials and colonists viewed impoverished herders and the hunters, whom they called 'robbers', as predators. It is not known precisely when they began to exterminate San men and capture the women and children who could more easily be 'tamed' as servants. The first recorded case of the extermination of men is in 1731. In 1715 the control of commandos had passed from the Company to the burgher militia. These commandos enabled colonists to expand their labour supply. Throughout the century San captured in war (*krijgsgevangenes*), or simply kidnapped, were indentured to farmers with whom

Adam Kok I (c. 1710–1795) and his descendants: a Bastaard family

The first Adam Kok, founder of a leading Bastaard (later Griqua) family, was probably a manumitted slave with at least one European in his ancestry. At some point Kok moved to Piketberg, married, and acquired large herds and flocks.

The order of events in his life is not clear. When Kok was granted grazing rights on the farm Stinkfontein in 1751, he was described as a 'Hottentot'. This suggests that he already had a following of local herders – the Chariguriqua, or Guriqua – who had, according to familiar practice, attached themselves to a successful pastoralist. Although he was granted burgher rights, he apparently received the staff of office by which the Company recognised its allies among the indigenous chiefs. His son Cornelis told John Campbell of the London Missionary Society that he had inherited this staff and had exchanged it for a British staff after the change of government in 1795.

Adam Kok I migrated to the Kamiesberg in Little Namaqualand. There Cornelis became a man of substance, holding several farms, and both were influential in regional affairs. People who acted as middlemen in trade, especially trade in ivory, between the southern

Tswana and the colony could become wealthy. Pastoralists of substance, like the Koks, could afford the weapons, ammunition and wagons needed for commercial hunting and trade.

From around 1780 some of the Koks and Barends, another well-off Bastaard family, settled along the Orange River. They may have gone there because of increasing pressure on colonial land as well as for the trade advantages of that locality. Cornelis and his large following only moved across the Orange later on, but Adam Kok I is said to have died near the Orange River in 1795. His grandson, Adam Kok II, and later generations of Koks were to become prominent in Griqua politics and social life.

The Koks, Barends and other Bastaards behaved much as the trekboers of the same period behaved. If the San, Tswana, or Nama and Kora (the Khoikhoi of the lower and middle Orange) resisted their invasion of the territory they inhabited, they formed commandos to chastise them. They, too, lived in extended family units with assorted dependants, governed by senior men. Their preferred lifestyle was pastoral: livestock wealth was the foundation of independence. They formed alliances in times of need, in preference to settled government.

Some Bastaards learned to read and write, and were baptised. A few attained burgher status and received grants of land. But all lost out in contests over land where Europeans were involved. They were most unhappy· when, towards the end of the century, they were targeted for military service with the Khoikhoi and 'Bastaard-Hottentots', which they saw as a loss of social standing.

they had to remain for life. Some Khoikhoi took part in these raids, but increasingly as servants of the burghers, rather than as allies.

When the settlers invaded their areas, some of the herders responded by moving out of their way. For example, certain Cochoqua, who became known as 'Gunjemans' (after their chief, Gonnema), were found later in the century at widely separated points, such as the Orange River and the eastern Cape. Some so-called Bushmen who fiercely resisted trekboer expansion to the north were herders who had lost their pastures and cattle nearer to Table Bay.

Some of the dislocated Khoikhoi went on to take the land and cattle of other herders. The Bastaards, who were people of mixed descent (mainly Khoikhoi and European, at first), spearheaded expansion into Namaqualand from the 1730s, at a time when many trekboers were taking a more easterly route. The Bastaards lived very like the Dutch and many were baptised. The pattern in their case was one of fairly easy access to land so long as this did not cause serious inconvenience to the white farmers. Baptised Bastaards of Namaqualand and other remote spots, such as the Zwartberg and the Koup, were able to register their farms. Some families prospered – most notably the Koks (see box). Later in the century, when there was more pressure on the land, colonial Bastaards felt their position slip. They became more closely identified in legal, social and military terms with the Khoikhoi and the offspring of slave–Khoikhoi unions, known as Bastaard-Hottentots. From around 1780, many of these people crossed the Orange River in an attempt to continue as pastoralists and escape colonial controls.

In his research Nigel Penn not only tackled the written records, but explored the mountains, grasslands and semi-arid zones where Cape hunters and herders had lived. What he found from this two-pronged approach was that conflict increased when there was a period of environmental crisis. When pressure on the regions best supplied with water and pastures increased, the Khoikhoi struggled to limit the colonists' access to these resources, and the colonists struggled to expel the Khoikhoi or reduce their share. After several such conflicts where the Khoikhoi lost out, they mounted a prolonged defence that lasted for much of the 1700s: 'The most violent Khoisan resistance to colonial expansion occurred along an important environmental frontier … [trekboer] expansion into the interior in the north-western Cape remained stalled along the dividing line between the winter and summer rainfall regions for over a hundred years.'

Penn has shown the ups and downs of this relationship. The colonists oppressed or protected the Khoikhoi to serve their own land and labour interests as they saw them at a given time. Similarly, the Khoikhoi resisted or co-operated according to how they saw their options. Herder co-operation with the European pastoralists is sometimes called 'collaboration'. This implies a betrayal of group welfare by some individuals for purely selfish ends. But is this fair – or correct? The historian Yvette Abrahams writes:

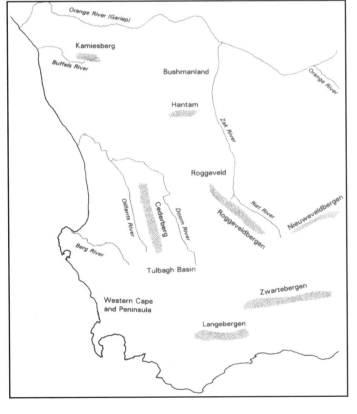

Figure 49. Nigel Penn has noted that: 'The most violent Khoisan resistance to colonial expansion occurred along an important environmental frontier – imprecise and shifting though it was – between the winter and summer rainfall regions of the Cape'. Pastoralists battled for control of the water sources vital for their stock. This map shows the regions where conflict between trekboer and Khoikhoi was most fierce. By contrast with the wet south-west, such areas as 'Bushmanland' are extremely arid.

[T]his issue has particular resonance in an account of Khoisan history, since it is striking how often collaboration and resistance are united in the same person. To write of these people as if they were one and not the other is to give a highly skewed picture of history. Moreover, we cannot understand their lives, their motives or their actions. In Khoisan history, the part of the collaborator was no less dangerous, and often less rewarding, than that of the guerilla. Autjoema [Autshumato], for instance, has often been called the first collaborator, yet he was also the first political prisoner on Robben Island ... When Khoisan motives are brought into the picture, even the most cursory consideration of collaboration reveals it to be much more than an easy option, but one of a range of tactics deployed in the broader struggle to understand and resist colonialism. This is not surprising if we assume that the Khoisan were unwilling (and in later centuries often unable) to turn to violence except as a last resort.

Eastern Cape

Valuable information concerning the indigenous people of the eastern Cape was recorded by C. A. Haupt, diarist for the important fact-gathering expedition undertaken by Ensign A. F. Beutler in 1752. The expeditions of Cruse and Schrijver (see p. 69), the Beutler expedition, and the oral traditions compiled by both the Xhosa historian J. H. Soga and the German missionary A. Kropf, are the major sources for the history of this region before the arrival of the trekboers. On the basis of these and other records, and of linguistic evidence, it seems clear that Khoikhoi and Xhosa interacted at many levels. These included intermarriage, trade, policy concerns and patron–client relationships (where roles depended upon who required the protection of whom). Indeed, Gerrit Harinck has claimed that 'we cannot properly speak of a "frontier" between Xhosa and Khoikhoi societies'. From this mingling came the Gonaqua, who followed Khoikhoi language and custom, and the Gqunukhwebe chiefdom, which followed more closely the Xhosa social structure and lifestyle.

The Beutler expedition in the 1750s observed the desperate plight of most eastern Khoikhoi, many of whom no longer knew 'of what nation they were'. They had been weakened by wars and had lost their livestock through the robberies of the San. Here again the boundaries between Khoikhoi and San appear to have blurred, since cattleless herders often joined the 'Bushmen' bands. Although the easternmost settler farm was 'Hagel-kraal', at the foot of the Attaquas Pass near Mossel Bay, the colonists had made their presence felt through hunting and trading long before. By 1752 many places which the Beutler expedition reached already had Dutch names, for example the Zwartkops, Sondags and Boesmans rivers. From the 1770s, parties of Europeans regularly toured the region and trekboers arrived in the Sneeuwberg, the Camdeboo and the coastal district east of the Gamtoos. The claims of surviving Khoikhoi clans to decent pastures were ignored: in 1770 some officials ordered a Khoikhoi on the Gamtoos 'to decamp with his cattle, and return to his old place, as he had too many cattle, and thus injured the pasture

Ruyter/Kohla/Toena, captain of the Hoengiqua of the eastern Cape

On 29 May 1752 the Beutler expedition met Captain Ruyter and his Hoengiqua. One specialist in Khoikhoi languages thinks the name 'Hoengiqua' has some connection with beards and hairiness. Ruyter had formed the Hoengiqua by uniting remnants of pastoral groups with himself as chief. European travellers sometimes confused the Hoengiqua with the Gonaqua, a neighbouring group, but Ruyter insisted that they were not the same.

Ruyter travelled with Beutler from the Blaauwkrantz River, where they met, as far as the Keiskamma River. He claimed to control the area between the Damasonqua country and that point, but the party's official map shows his territory between the Kariega and the Great Fish rivers. Anders Sparrman, the Swedish naturalist, named the area at the mouth of the Great Fish River 'Koning Ruyter's Craal' in 1776, while Robert Jacob Gordon, commander of the Dutch garrison, found him west of the Fish in 1778.

Ruyter explained to Beutler that, to safeguard their cattle from San robbers, the Hoengiqua placed them amongst the herds of friendly Xhosa chiefs. We know of one dispute which arose out of arrangements such as this (see below). Relations between Khoikhoi and Xhosa on the eastern frontier were very complex, and historians struggle to make sense of numerous confusing and contradictory accounts.

Sparrman tells an involved tale of murder and escape which brought Ruyter to the eastern frontier from a farm in the Roggeveld. In fact Sparrman never met Ruyter, but took the story from 'several Christians' who claimed to know him. Although most historians have called Ruyter a Khoikhoi, some who base their descriptions on Sparrman's account have called him an escaped slave. George Stow states that he was the 'last Bushman captain' of the region, who used bows and poisoned arrows against the Xhosa with much success. His names tell us much about the mingling which was taking place: he explained to Gordon that his Khoikhoi name was Toena, that the Xhosa called him 'Coosjo' (Kohla), while he was Ruyter to the Dutch.

Sparrman's story of Ruyter's early career has raised questions. As Susan Newton-King points out, Beutler 'recorded Ruiter's amazement at the sight of a mirror and a "brand-glas", which he must surely have encountered before, had he been in service' to a Roggeveld colonist.

Beutler gave Ruyter a copper escutcheon with the Company's mark engraved on it. As an official captain, he was expected to act in the Company's interests. Later travellers commented on this. Sparrman writes of Ruyter as being cruel in his manner of ruling but 'a true and faithful ally': a buffer between the Xhosa and the colonists, and their assistant in the business of making 'slaves' of 'straggling Boshies-men'. Gordon reported that Ruyter had a 'polite manner and very pleasant appearance'. He assured him that the governor 'liked him very much because he had always been a good chief'.

Sparrman believed that Ruyter's following had shrunk to around 200, and that he had become a pathetic beggar by

1776. Yet some who followed, for example Gordon, provide more positive accounts. The English botanist and soldier William Paterson reported in 1779 that Ruyter had just defeated some Xhosa in a fight. After this, the history of the Hoengiqua is unclear: probably they were the 'Giqua' known to have been absorbed by some Xhosa at a somewhat later date.

Ruyter's grandchildren became involved in the dispute mentioned above, in which the Gqunukhwebe claimed that they had given the Hoengiqua cattle in exchange for territorial rights between the Bushman and the Fish rivers in the 1760s. This dispute reflects the importance of the Zuurveld for pastoralists and underlines Ruyter's stand to assert Khoikhoi claims to it.

Figure 50. Ruyter, Hoengiqua chief and grandfather of Ruiter Beesje (by R. J. Gordon 1788).

In the 1700s Ruyter collected Khoikhoi from broken clans near the Great Fish River and formed a new group, the Hoengiqua. The Dutch gave a copper breastplate bearing the Company emblem to Chief Ruyter. This gesture meant that they regarded him as their ally. The Company treated the Hoengiqua as a buffer; that is, a neutral or friendly force between the Xhosa and the trekboers who were pushing ever further east.

Figure 51. Ruiter Beesje (known also as Benedictus Platje Ruyter), a Gonaqua captain (by H. J. Klein, 1802).

Much had changed by the time Captain Ruiter Beesje became the leader. The Hoengiqua had not survived as an independent group, some merging with the Xhosa and others with the Gonaqua. Captain Ruiter was paid by the government to find recruits for the Cape Corps, the Khoikhoi regiment. His claim to be the rightful owner of the Zuurveld was dismissed.

These pictures clearly show changes in the status and lifestyles of the two men.

of the inhabitants'. A noteworthy attempt by dispersed Khoikhoi to regroup and defend their resources came about through the efforts of Ruyter.

Missions in the 1700s

The Company continued to keep a small number of clergymen at the Cape but, almost without exception, they neglected the Khoikhoi and San. Since church and state were united in the Company, there was no way other denominations could do evangelical work. In 1737 a Moravian missionary was allowed to work among some Hessequa. He made a deep impression on several of his flock, but when he baptised them he met with official opposition, and soon left the Cape.

Exclusion of other churches and neglect by the Dutch affected the indigenous population more than at first appears. The Dutch church required that its communicants be able to read: the only schools were those supported by the church, but the Khoikhoi and San were not drawn into these. Burghership, and hence burgher rights, were available only to Christians. This exclusion also affected the way evidence before the courts was received, since non-Christians were supposed not to be bound, as Christians were, by the oath to tell the truth. This was not just a matter of prejudice, but an authentic legal issue, which crops up later in official documents. When some Khoikhoi complained that the War of 1739 was caused by certain colonists, it was objected that the Company paid too much heed to the word of 'unbaptised Hottentots'. In 1780 the Company allowed the Lutherans to establish a church and in 1792 the Moravians renewed their mission to the Hessequa. With the British takeover in 1795, the door was opened to fresh ideas: four evangelists of the London Missionary Society arrived in 1799 and other societies were soon active at the Cape.

Khoikhoi converts in the 1700s

Fredrik Adolf: Khoikhoi language teacher and early convert

The Revd Petrus Kalden who came as minister to the Cape in 1695 showed a rare enthusiasm for missionary work. In 1697 he told the Classis of Amsterdam (presbytery of the Dutch Reformed Church) that he wished to convert the heathen. More remarkably, he felt the right approach was to speak to the Khoikhoi in their own language. When the Revd François Valentyn made his third visit to the Cape in 1705 he found that the Khoikhoi man who was teaching Kalden to speak 'Hottentot' had gained an impressive understanding of Christian theology.

Kalden's efforts were cut short when he became a target of the burgher revolt which unseated W. A. van der Stel. He had to leave the Cape in 1708, and took with him his Khoikhoi assistant. This man was baptised Fredrik Adolf at a church at Vianen, in the Netherlands, in 1709. It is not clear when he returned to the Cape, but the reported sequel is that he behaved so immorally that he was banished to Robben Island, where he died.

We don't have the information to be able to understand fully the story of Fredrik Adolf, but we do know some of the attitudes that might have shaped his life: Valentyn wrote of Kalden's success as a Christian teacher as amazing, since his pupil was Khoikhoi – 'the most savage, stupid and filthy heathens I had ever met'. In reporting on their work, the missionaries often stressed the depravity of people whom they 'saved'. Like Valentyn, himself a churchman, they measured their success against their own social stereotypes. Valentyn believed that God would richly reward Dutch efforts to bring these people to the light.

Vehettge Tikkuie, called 'Magdalena': the first Khoikhoi evangelist

One of the most astonishing stories in mission history is that of 'Lena', a Moravian convert who was probably a Hessequa.

In 1737 George Schmidt, a Moravian from Saxony, was permitted to preach the gospel to 'Hottentots'. He spent the next seven years amongst the Khoikhoi near modern Caledon, at a place which was later called Genadendal.

In his journal Schmidt mentioned both Vehettge Tikkuie and her husband Jaktie but, of the two, Vehettge responded more warmly to his teachings. It seems that her ability to read, write and receive religious instruction caused a rift with the other women, and with Jaktie, which was a source of stress. On several occasions she left and returned to her parents' home for weeks or even months. She knew that her actions there could never meet with Schmidt's approval, and this was likely to have been another source of tension in her life.

Vehettge Tikkuie's conversion took place in April 1742 when she was christened Magdalena by Schmidt. Conver-

sion meant a life of piety and other-worldliness, Christian morality and hard work. This was a big change from life as a pastoralist and practitioner of Khoikhoi religious beliefs. Records show that Schmidt had little understanding of the spiritual and personal problems his converts faced (he had baptised several others at around the same time) and saw the doubts and questions which they raised as threats to his teachings and himself.

Clergy and officials reacted strongly to the baptisms, and Schmidt, who had been lonely and frustrated in his work in any case, decided to leave the Cape in October 1743, until the problems could be sorted out.

On Christmas Eve in 1792, the first Moravian missionaries in 50 years met Magdalena near the spot where Schmidt had worked. She had kept her New Testament. The three missionaries learned that she had prayed and read from the scriptures throughout and involved other Khoikhoi in her worship, just as Schmidt had hoped his converts might. She died in January 1800 and still awaits the recognition that she clearly earned as South Africa's first woman evangelist. Schmidt had struggled to attract a following, but later missionaries faced a rush of applicants. The Khoikhoi had become much poorer and their social structures were much weaker, which favoured later missionary work.

Dispossession and subordination

Recent studies of slavery at the Cape have helped researchers to understand colonial attitudes to labour, and the position of groups who were neither masters nor slaves (for example, the Khoikhoi, Bastaards, and small communities of immigrants). It has been useful to compare the Cape with other places where slaves and free labour worked side by side. Problems arose, in the eyes of the colonists, from the fact of children born of slave liaisons with the free Khoikhoi, whom they were not entitled to enslave. In 1721 some burghers in Stellenbosch demanded the right to indenture (*inboek*) these children, whom they called 'Bastaard-Hottentots'. The Council of Policy did not introduce a formal *inboekstelsel* until 1775 but the practice of tying 'free' children to the farms evidently began informally around this time.

The duty of freeburghers to render military service was extended to other categories of society in the 1700s. In 1722 the small category of 'free blacks', most of whom were manumitted slaves, formed a separate militia company under 'free black' officers. From the 1770s the obligation of free persons (but not slaves) to defend the state was enforced also on the Bastaards, Bastaard-Hottentots and Khoikhoi. Although they carried out this burgher duty, they still lacked full citizenship, or 'burgher rights'. The Khoikhoi regiment had skills which made them better suited to service at the Cape than any other group. However, many colonists doubted their loyalty and resented the fact that military service robbed the farms of workers. The first unit, formed in 1781, was soon dis-

Figure 52. In 1802, when this drawing of a Khoikhoi soldier was made, the Cape Corps was billeted at Rietvlei, north of Cape Town (near modern Milnerton). Note the tents in the background.

banded but the unit formed in 1793 became the Cape Corps (or Regiment), which rendered many years of service. The regiment had European officers, except for those of non-commissioned rank.

Recent research tries to answer questions about economic developments in the 1700s. How did the Dutch East India Company's blend of government and commerce function at the Cape? How did the colony's merchants, grain and

Figure 53. The figure of a young Hottentot in his regimentals (no shoes) lectured by his Corporal for some little inadvertancy ... their young Colonel seems very much attached to them and vain of their improvements as we are of having made good children of naughty ones.' This drawing by Lady Anne Barnard is one of a series depicting the people she observed at the Cape. Her comment is interesting.

wine producers fit into the world economy? How important was the Cape meat market to distant pastoralists? Were market opportunities as important as other factors which caused the trekboers to make the Khoikhoi work for them, and encroach on their water, pastures and hunting grounds? The documents are most detailed for periods of warfare or unusual stress. Historians are interested to know if the best-documented hostilities (those of 1739, and 1754–5 in the north; of 1770–*c.* 1798 over an immense area to the north and north-east; and of 1799–1803 on the eastern frontier) were mainly local in origin or if they could be traced to external forces. Likewise, the newer studies of Khoikhoi and San in the interior have added to our understanding of the motive and the scope of their resistance to the colonists' advance.

The harsh reality of racism in the past hundred years imposes itself on any exploration of southern Africa's past. Was the discrimination which is evident in the historical records of the 1700s due to ideas of 'race'? The revulsion which marked some early descriptions of the indigenous people of the Cape is matched in the 1700s by resentment and disgust, for example, concerning 'racial' mixing. 'There is no trusting the blood of Ham,' asserted some wealthy burghers of Stellenbosch in 1706, referring to 'Kaffirs, Mulattoes, Mesticos, Casticos and all that black brood living among us, who have been bred from marriages and other forms of mingling'. It became fairly common for colonists to denounce officials who took account of Khoikhoi requests and complaints as 'Hottentot landdrosts', or 'Hottentot heemraden'; one was even described as 'King of the

Hottentots'. Moreover, the fear was expressed that Europeans were at risk through constant contact with slaves and Khoikhoi, especially since they often lacked the 'civilising' influences of education and church.

Also present in the documents is evidence for interdependence. This involved adaptation and cultural exchanges between groups. Historians studying these documents have to account for the fact that, in spite of these exchanges, separation on grounds of 'race' became a guiding principle in politics. There has been much discussion about the role of Calvinist theology, of the 'frontier' mentality, and of colour, culture and class, in the process which secured economic and political privilege for one section of the population. The way in which colonists saw and treated people different from themselves was influenced by the ideological baggage they brought with them, by the new thinking in Europe which slowly reached the Cape, and by their own experiences in the colonies. This makes a discussion of the factors which structured the social hierarchy extremely complex.

Figure 54. Here a Dutch sailor (note the flag) is shown in a romantic pose with a young Khoikhoi woman.

New forces at work: the 1800s

8

Between 1795 and 1814 the Cape changed hands three times: from the Dutch East India Company to British rule in 1795, from British to Batavian rule in 1803, and back to Britain in 1806 – confirmed by the London Convention of 1814 at the end of the Napoleonic wars. In spite of all these changes, there was a marked degree of continuity. For example, we can look at regulations governing labour at the Cape. Protection of the Khoikhoi worker began with a register of hire contracts introduced in Graaff-Reinet in 1799. This measure, a response to the widespread rebellion in the eastern districts, affected only about 400 workers before it lapsed. A connecting thread in later measures such as the contract systems of the Batavians (1803) and the British (1809), and the child indenture proclamations (1812, 1817, 1819), was the subordination-with-protection of servants.

During the First British Occupation, Samuel Daniell, an artist, visited the Cape. He was the first to draw pictures on the spot, and also oversee their reproduction in Europe. However, by the 1800s misinformation about the Khoikhoi and San had created an image of them which prepared the ground for a bizarre venture in exploiting a curiosity

Figure 55. T'Kaness, 'the daughter of T'Goosht Kaba, a wealthy chief of the Korah Hottentots' was sketched by Samuel Daniell while north of the Gariep in 1801–2. He wrote: 'Her skin was as fair as that of a European. She was the most timid of all the natives who were met with on the expedition.' Daniell was a professional artist and his drawings of the indigenous people are without the usual tendency to caricature.

of nature. As one writer remarks, 'anyone of that day who had heard anything at all about Hottentots' would 'read between the lines' and recognise the joke intended by an advertisement which announced the opportunity to view "The Hottentot Venus", newly arrived in England from 'the interior of South Africa'. Saartje Baartman's appearance seemed to confirm the widely held belief that 'Hottentots' were a subhuman species native to the African continent (see box).

British administration

With the influx of British merchants, soldiers, travellers and missionaries, information about people at the Cape increased dramatically. The tax enumeration of 1798 provided official data about the stock holdings of Khoikhoi living on burgher farms not available from earlier *opgaafs*. In Cape Town, in 1800, three *opgaaf* lists were prepared to separate out former Company servants, other European residents, and a category comprising Bastaards, 'Hottentots' and free blacks. Such documents display a desire for system and can be used to trace, among other things, the evolution of race consciousness. The new government lacked immediate experience of the Cape. The British called for reports to bring them up to date. These reports are valuable sources of information, for example W. S. van Ryneveld's *Plan for Amending the Interior Police* (1801) with its perspectives on 'Peasant' (the Dutch farmers) and 'Hottentot'.

Short-term residents and travellers, such as John Barrow and Lady Anne Barnard during the first British occupation, Hinrich Lichtenstein of the Batavian period, and William Burchell after 1806, made rich contributions in terms of comment and minutely observed detail. In 1797, Barrow claimed that there were no remaining independent settlements of Khoikhoi in the vast new district of Graaff-Reinet. In the colony as a whole, there were a few captains with small bands of followers, but their independence was considerably reduced by the terms on which they received staffs of office from the government. The return of the Moravian mission in late 1792, and the arrival of London Missionary

Saartje Baartman, the 'Hottentot Venus'

The 'perfect Specimen' of a Khoikhoi female who died in Paris after five years (1810–15) on exhibition – as a freak – was said to have been born on the 'Banks of the River Gamtoos'. By her own account, she left there when young and worked as nursemaid for Hendrik Cezar, a farmer near Cape Town. Cezar and a British surgeon had formed a speculative partnership. They took her to London where they charged admission for the opportunity to view what they described as 'this extraordinary phenomena of nature'.

Saartje's steatopygous buttocks were the most visible curiosity, but the public was titillated by news of a genital peculiarity, the so-called 'Hottentot apron'. Steatopygia refers to the tendency in some women for fat to accumulate on the hips and buttocks, rather than the abdomen or elsewhere. When Saartje moved, this mass of tissue trembled and shook. Her striking features were compared to the European norm, and gave rise to theories that her people had peculiar ideas of feminine beauty and were closer on the 'great chain of being' to apes than human beings.

Some viewers were offended and outraged. They saw a helpless creature being degraded and exploited for profit. Prominent humanitarians took her handlers to court. A judge arranged for Saartje to be interviewed in the Low Dutch language which she could understand.

But according to the affidavit which her interviewers signed, Saartje claimed that she herself had gone with Cezar to obtain permission to travel to England for the purpose of exhibiting herself; that she was treated well; and that, although she did not fully understand her contract, she knew she should receive part of the proceeds from their show and was entirely satisfied. In view of this, the judge dismissed the case.

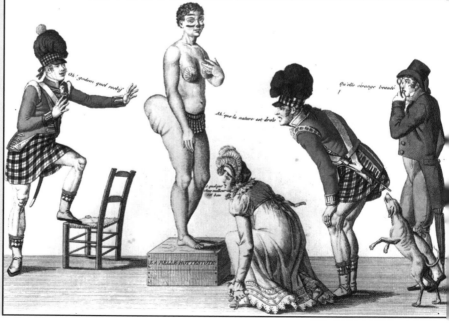

Figure 56. Saartje Baartman was exhibited in Britain and France during her life and remained an object of curiosity long after her death in Paris in 1815. This French engraving is titled 'The curious in ecstasy at the shoelaces'.

Saartje died in Paris in 1815 when, by her own reckoning, she was under thirty years of age. Her body was dissected by the French comparative anatomist, Georges Cuvier, who collected and studied specimens from all over the world.

The 'Hottentot Venus' added to the negative perceptions which the Khoikhoi have endured at scientific and popular levels. Her physical appearance, which was an extreme case of a condition by no means common, resulted in generalisations still referred to today. Saartje appears as a grotesque and repellent figure in surviving doggerel verse and cartoons, always with the name 'Hottentot' (or, sometimes, 'Bushman') attached. The very court which heard her case believed that 'the Hottentot nation' required the Cape governor's protection 'by reason of their general imbecile state'.

Society representatives in 1799, marked the start of detailed mission records. Before long, missionaries from the Wesleyan church and other sects were also in the field.

In his 1801 report, Van Ryneveld made the point that no Hottentots should 'be suffered to remain within the Boundaries of this Colony' unless they worked for farmers, were members of the 'licensed kraals' (independent villages) or lived at 'the [schools] lately established here by the Missionaries'. A fourth category of legitimacy was still taking shape as successive governments wavered on the point of disbanding or expanding the unit of Khoikhoi and Bastaard soldiers. In 1806 it was made a British line regiment, for service only at the Cape. Before and after this event, the records contain many references to how and why this regiment was used, and what the costs were to the Cape government.

It is clear that by this time San and Khoikhoi independence was a thing of the past. An unknown number of colonial Khoikhoi preferred to live among the Xhosa where, it appears, their knowledge of the colony and expertise with guns made them welcome, if still subordinate. Others fled across the Orange River or chose an insecure existence, often dependent on banditry, in the wilder recesses of the Cape.

The Khoikhoi's system of government

Figure 57. In 1803, three Christian converts of the London Missionary Society missionary James Kicherer travelled to England and the Netherlands. They were Maria and Johannes van Rooy and Martha Arendse.

which revolved around clan 'captains' and supra-clan 'chiefs' had disintegrated or become distorted in the 1600s in the south-western Cape. This process continued at an accelerated rate in the 1700s. Increasingly, captaincy was linked with the interests of local whites. For example, Khoikhoi captains were likely to be drawn from among those who served as agents for the recruitment of labour, or those who rendered valuable commando service. Captains were appointed by the Commander-in-Chief of the garrison at the Cape, although in practice, it was alleged, they were often nominated by colonists. The Khoikhoi rebellion of 1799–1803 saw a revival of captaincy in a form closer to the traditional mould. These leaders emerged among deserters from frontier farms where fair-sized family groups of Khoikhoi were preserved. The story of the Stuurman brothers begins with this development and spans the period during which captains became government servants.

Klaas, David, Andries and Bootsman Stuurman: the evolution of Khoikhoi captaincy, 1799–1809

The Stuurman brothers (and sisters, of whom little is known) were born at a spot said to have been 'reserved for the Hottentots' at the Gamtoos River mouth. It was given on loan to a farmer by Governor Van Plettenberg in 1778 and the Stuurmans took service with the trekboers then arriving in ever greater numbers in the eastern Cape.

Klaas and David were among the hundreds of servants who deserted the farms early in 1799 after British and Khoikhoi troops arrived on the frontier to suppress an insurrection of frontier farmers. Some deserters crossed the colonial boundary and went to live with the Xhosa, but in April a large group approached the British commander to ask for protection. Klaas Stuurman was their spokesperson and his declaration of Khoikhoi grievances and hopes was recorded by John Barrow. However, rumours of bad faith soon made the Stuurman party also join the Xhosa. A war, in which the colony confronted a Khoikhoi–Xhosa alliance, began in May.

The 'rebel captains' and their followers formed bases in the Zuurveld where they held out until the war ended in 1803. Some farm deserters fled to the village of Graaff-Reinet where H. C. D. Maynier, a former landdrost, was charged with the task of pacifying the district. Maynier organised the refugees under captains, some of whom he appointed himself. These captains were answerable to the government. They trusted this government to protect them from the 'masters' they had left. Under pressure from the white inhabitants to disperse, some enrolled in the Cape Corps (the Khoikhoi regiment) and were sent to Cape Town. Most of the rest followed the London Missionary Society (LMS) missionaries James Read and J. T. van der Kemp to a farm near Algoa Bay which, the government hoped, would be a magnet to the Zuurveld rebels. On the night of 27 September 1802 the mission station was attacked by a party led, as it turned out, by Andries Stuurman, whose dead body was discovered the next day.

Some surviving rebels went into exile, but most returned to the farms or took up two new options: enrolment in a mission 'school' or in the Khoikhoi regiment. Klaas alone received a copper breastplate (bearing the words 'Klaas Stuurman, Captain of the Hottentots, Peace and Friendship with the Batavian Republic') and a farm near his childhood home. When Klaas died in a hunting accident, David was named captain and led a party of 42, of whom Bootsman was one, onto the land in March 1804.

As captain, David was expected to supply men for any service required by government officials. He was also called on for recruits for the Cape Regiment. After 1806 the new British government formalised its links with Khoisan leaders, distributing staffs of office more widely than before. The landdrost of Uitenhage reported in 1808 that Stuurman refused to fetch his staff after 'a trifling difference' with a recruiting officer.

From the start, relations between the Stuurman party and their Boer neighbours had been strained. In 1809, a time of growing tension on the frontier, the community was broken up: David, Bootsman and two other men, together with three women and seven children, were arrested and marched to Cape Town as prisoners, on the grounds of 'suspicious conduct, living in a Kraal near the boundaries of the Colony'. The men, who were placed on Robben Island, soon escaped and made their way to 'Xhosaland' where they remained for many years.

The government then abolished the captains' remaining powers. The same proclamation (1 November 1809), which regulated labour, 'removed all vestige of chieftainship from the Hottentots in the colony'. The Khoikhoi, like other inhabitants, were from then on answerable to the local colonial authorities – the Fiscal, the district landdrost and the veldcoronets.

Captains were, however, retained to perform certain tasks, especially with regard to the Cape Regiment. For many years the colony's accounts showed items such as 'Pay of Hottentot Captains for the purpose of encouraging them to promote the enlistment of recruits from their respective Kraals'. With justice, it was said that David Stuurman had been the 'last chief' of the Khoikhoi.

Cultural changes

When a community is conquered, changes in cultural practices such as their religion, language and marriage customs, usually result. The herders adopted the Dutch language and, sometimes, Portuguese, well ahead of other indicators of cultural change. This was due partly to the difficulty Europeans had at first in learning the click languages of the Khoikhoi and San. Lichtenstein, a physician and naturalist who lived at the Cape from 1803 to 1806, wrote that Dutch was the language of the colonial Khoikhoi and their own language was spoken only by people still-independent beyond the frontier.

The missionaries promoted cultural change. Van der Kemp produced a Gonaqua catechism merely as an interim aid. He assumed that it would serve their interests to speak Dutch in the longer term. All the same, 'native' catechists who were trained by the eastern Cape missions were valued for their command of one or more indigenous languages. The Revd John Campbell of the LMS heard Andries Stoffels, a Gona, recite the Lord's Prayer in his native tongue. James Backhouse, a Quaker visitor in 1839, reported a complex situation where 'an old Hottentot, named Bootsman Stuurman, preached in his harsh native language … and another person interpreted into Caffer for the benefit of the Fingoes and Gonas. The old Hottentot afterwards addressed the company in Dutch.' To the north, Nama became the subject of a pioneering linguistic study in the late 1800s and still survives as a living language. South Africa, with its many spoken languages, has needed interpreters from the time of Autshumato and Krotoa to the present day.

Our understanding of cultural change among the Khoikhoi requires interpretation of an immense volume of records. We have to remember that, in the course of interaction, all parties are to some extent transformed. Christian missions were only one of the catalysts of change. Interaction on the farms, in the commandos, in the Cape Regiment and elsewhere, had a strong transforming power. Much of the interaction took place 'in a frontier zone, where, by definition, a decisive struggle for political power is taking place'. Overall, the mission

Bretagne Jantjes: Khoikhoi interpreter in the early 1800s

Bretagne Jantjes, a Gonaqua, was born in the 1760s between the Sundays and Great Fish rivers. After the Khoikhoi's war of independence of 1799–1803 he worked for a farmer at Algoa Bay and then entered Bethelsdorp mission in 1806. As a tanner and a wagon owner, he was among the more independent of the mission Khoikhoi. He testified in a number of cases which came before the circuit court through the efforts of James Read and Dr Van der Kemp. Landdrost Cuyler of Uitenhage relied on Jantjes a great deal and sent him on many errands requiring courage and diplomacy. The missionaries also gave him important tasks. His knowledge of the people, terrain and languages of the frontier proved a lifelong asset to him.

On 2 April 1817, when the governor Lord Charles Somerset met the Xhosa chief Ngqika at the Kat River, Jantjes was one of the interpreters. Because so many languages – Dutch, English, Xhosa, Gona – were spoken, and such important issues were at stake, all the parties brought interpreters that they could trust. There were two officials who spoke Dutch and English, two Dutch colonists who understood Xhosa, and two Gona, Jantjes and Hendrik Nootka, who carried out the Dutch–Xhosa and Xhosa–Dutch translations. Not long after this, when the fifth frontier war broke out, Jantjes served as interpreter for the Bethelsdorp Khoikhoi who were recruited into the colonial force.

In his old age (1836), Jantjes was interviewed by Donald Moodie. He spoke about his youth. Jantjes remembered that the Xhosa and Khoikhoi had lived peaceably before the trekboers reached the Zuurveld, upsetting this equilibrium and the herders' way of life.

Figure 58. 'Hottentot Waggon-driver'. Visitors to the Cape were amazed at the numbers of oxen yoked to wagons and the Khoikhoi wagon-drivers' skill in controlling them, by wielding immensely long whips.

records afford the richest source of insights into conscious efforts on all sides, including the evangelical movement, the government, colonists and local officials, and the Khoikhoi themselves, to shape, hasten and control the process of cultural change.

Missionaries in the early 1800s

The missionaries who began their work in the early 1800s acquired land by means of government grants given under tickets of occupation. Genadendal, Groenekloof (Mamre), Bethelsdorp and Theopolis were missions of this type. In other cases societies bought tracts which could be enlarged as neighbouring farms came on the market. In this way the Moravians acquired Elim and Wittewater (Enon), the LMS Hankey, the Rhenish Wupperthal and Steinthal, and so forth. Baptism, the main issue which forced George Schmidt to retire in 1744, was now allowed. Indigenous people, or slaves, who had been baptised were seldom called Christians, as that signified attributes of full citizenship which they were not eligible to acquire before their 'emancipation'.

The Batavians tried to ensure that the missionaries would mould a docile underclass. In 1803 they forbade the LMS at Bethelsdorp to teach reading or writing and extended this prohibition to the Bastaards of Klaarwater, an LMS settlement across the Orange, in 1805. In practice, however, these prohibitions may have been ignored. The government wanted any education the Khoikhoi received to enhance their usefulness as servants. Many colonists feared that servants might become more literate or versed in Christian doctrine than themselves. Cupido Kakkerlak provides a striking case of Christian converts in the early 1800s who, backed by the missionaries, tried to rise from servitude to middle-class respectability (see box).

By 1800 the northern Khoikhoi and San were interspersed with Bastaard immigrants. Generally the Bastaards became the dominant group. Before this happened, the Khoikhoi Chief Haaimaap (whom the colonists called Jantje Wildschut) invited the Wesleyan Methodist Missionary Society to send someone to his people at Leliefontein in the Kamiesberg. The missionary Barnabas Shaw described the 'council' on 15 October 1816 where 'Chief Haimaap fell with his

Figure 59. 'Patriarchal rule. Missionary and worker in the mission garden at Genadendal.' [This caption is from B. Kruger The Pear Tree Blossoms] The Moravian village of Genadendal is near Caledon in the Overberg, Cape. Missionaries of all denominations felt a duty to encourage 'industry' instead of 'idleness', and agriculture in addition to pastoral pursuits.

Figure 60. By 1847 when this scene at Genadendal was painted by G. F. Angas, the missions were under serious threat. Numbers of slaves freed in 1838 had joined the old residents, who were mainly Khoikhoi, at the missions. The colonists wanted these people to be dispersed as servants among themselves.

Cupido Kakkerlak: farmhand, wagon-driver and sawyer, Christian convert and assistant missionary (c. 1760–c. 1824)

Cupido Kakkerlak appears in the hire contract register, introduced by Resident Commissioner Maynier in November 1799, first in the employ of landdrost Bresler and then of a colonist.

In April 1801 James Read and A. A. van der Lingen of the London Missionary Society arrived in Graaff-Reinet, and were soon joined by Dr J. T. van der Kemp. Cupido began to attend services conducted by these three evangelists.

He and his elder son, Vigilant, had been counted with Khoikhoi owning taxable property on the *opgaaf* list of 1798. His inclusion on the contract register kept by Maynier signifies that he had been a rebel, or else had come to Graaff-Reinet to lodge a complaint. His conversion to Christianity was swift: on 30 December 1801, Dr Van der Kemp baptised Cupido and several of his children in the Sundays River. His wife, Anna, was baptised later, at Bethelsdorp. The Kakkerlak family were among those who accompanied the missionaries to Algoa Bay in February 1802 and founded the first LMS mission on a farm called 'Botha's Place'. In June 1803 they moved to Bethelsdorp.

Cupido's name heads a list of mission residents compiled in 1809 at the request of the Cape government. In the first ten years of Bethelsdorp he came to the fore in mission work, becoming a deacon in 1807. He also advanced materially, as a sawyer at a time when timber was in demand. Although in his forties,

he attended the reading and writing school and became a reader (in Dutch) at Sunday services. In 1813 he was chosen to escort the Revd John Campbell, out from England to inspect LMS missions, on his tour of the colony and points beyond.

In 1814 Cupido became an elder and Read's assistant, and later that year was selected to serve as assistant missionary. Professing a call to Griquatown (formerly Klaarwater), he left Bethelsdorp in 1815. His wife Anna had died in 1811, and while in Griquatown he remarried. From there he was moved to Nokaneng, some distance from Kuruman, to work among the Korana. In 1820 when Campbell revisited the Cape, he met Cupido again and reported sympathetically upon his lonely mission among impoverished, wandering people whose dialect he was by then 'too far advanced in life' to learn. After six years among the Korana, Cupido was removed from his post. He disappears from the records soon after this.

Before Cupido left Bethelsdorp, Read wrote that 'the prejudice against Hott.' had been breached and 'our Brother Cupido was taken for the first time to dine at the table of an African [Boer] farmer'. This report, hopeful of a future without discrimination against 'Hottentots', reflects the expectations of a 'civilising mission'. Cupido's success was marked in terms of self-improvement, promotion in his chosen work, and economic advance. But such recognition as he got was confined largely to the mission world created by the LMS.

face on the ground … and the following questions were proposed':

Have you plenty of water, and a suitable place where gardens may be made, and cultivation attended to?

'Ja Mynheer.' (Yes, Sir)

As the Missionary and his wife cannot live without bread as you do, will you allow him to cultivate corn for his own use?

'Yes, wherever he pleases; the land is before you; you may choose.'

Will you allow him to keep cows, goats, oxen &c., for the use of the Mission?

'Yes, as many as he pleases.'

Will you assist in the erection of a place of public worship, where you may assemble to hear the word of God?

'Ja, Mynheer.'

As the Missionary cannot live in huts like yours, will you assist him to build a dwelling-house, to make gardens, and in doing any other work?

'Ja, Mynheer.'

Are you really willing and desirous to receive the Gospel or the Great Word?

'Ja, Mynheer.'

This question was answered first by the *Chief*; then by the *men* who sat near him; and after them, both *women* and *children* caught the answer and repeated, 'Ik ben gewillig, &c.' (I am willing to receive it, &c.)

It is interesting to visualise this scene and try to imagine the thoughts and feelings of those present. In 1825 the head was formally divested of his powers, which the government gave to the chief missionary in his stead.

At other stations in Little Namaqualand (Steinkopf, Komaggas, Concordia and Richtersveld) the Bastaards were already present among the Khoikhoi

Figure 61. C. D. Bell called these people Griquas when he sketched them in 1834. Some of the Griqua, who were of mixed Khoikhoi and Dutch origin, had adopted the lifestyle of the colonists, while others, like the ones depicted here, more nearly retained the clothing, weapons, and customs of the Khoikhoi.

Figure 62. This Bastaard of Griquatown resembles a frontier burgher in every respect except, perhaps, for the fact that he carries a knobkierie in addition to his gun.

colony: Oorlams, Topnaars, Bergenaars, 'Mantatees', and dislocated Xhosa, to name only some. Missionaries of the various sects had a great impact on many of these and affected their development in complex ways. As shown by the excerpt from Shaw's memoir, their writings provide historians with uniquely intimate scenes – but it is seldom easy to interpret what they mean.

Equality before the law

The struggle which certain missionaries waged to attain equality before the law for the Khoikhoi was a response to the many examples of abuse reported by farmworkers and the frontier rebels. Their efforts resulted, in 1811, in the institution of circuit court judges, who made periodic visits to the inland drostdies to administer justice in serious cases.

A number of charges laid by Khoikhoi against colonists were heard in 1812. The accused were unhappy about having to defend themselves against charges brought by servants, in the presence of their fellow farmers. The 1812 circuit has been called the 'Black Circuit' ever since. The feeling that 'there is no longer any justice for us ... from our courts', compared with the ways in which they interacted with the Khoikhoi in the past, caused resentment among some colonists.

The arrival from Britain in 1823 of a commission to investigate conditions at the Cape gave hope of further progress towards 'impartial justice' for the Colony's slaves and farmworkers. The Charter of Justice issued in London in 1827 laid the groundwork for a legal system based on English jurisprudence. The old district courts of landdrost and

when the missionaries arrived. These stations were much more extensive than most because of the arid landscape and the fact that European farmers were not yet present in large numbers when they were marked out.

The Bastaards of Namaqualand became known as 'Basters'. Some who crossed the middle Orange were renamed Griquas in 1813. Migrations had always taken place, but European colonisation accelerated the movement and break-up of existing groups. New communities came into being, in and beyond the heemraden were replaced by resident magistrates and clerks of the peace. Certain powers of the field cornets were taken away and a jury system was introduced. These reforms, which were effective from 1 January 1828, were important steps towards equal status for all 'free' persons at the Cape. However, the status of the Khoikhoi was untouched: they still lacked burgher rights, including, for example, the right to private ownership of land.

Ordinance 50 of 1828

During the 1820s the Cape government looked at the question of labour more closely. In Britain, the movement supporting the abolition of slaves was gaining ground. At the Cape, measures to improve conditions for slaves were coming into force; pressure for equal rights for 'free' Khoikhoi was increasing; and persons from beyond the Colony's boundaries were coming to work, although their status was unclear.

After 1825 the governor was assisted by a council and legislated by ordinance instead of by proclamation as before. In July 1828, two important ordinances were enacted. The first, Ordinance 49, introduced a pass system for foreigners (members of 'tribes' beyond the Colony) who were willing to enter into labour contracts for a year. The second, Ordinance 50, applied to 'Hottentots and other free persons of colour'. In their case, the pass system was abolished and at last they had the right to own land in the Colony. Dr John Philip of the London Missionary Society, who had campaigned for this reform, was disappointed that the ordinance was not 'colour blind'. On the other hand, he was

relieved when the British government inserted a clause protecting the ordinance from being changed or withdrawn without the consent of the Crown.

The records tell us little about Khoikhoi reactions when they heard the news. James Read of Bethelsdorp reported: 'The Hottentots of this place have not been much elated by hearing of the liberty; in fact, it will not so much affect them, except in the pass system, which is now done with.' A little later he observed that 'something more on the side of government was needed, that was to give land to the Hottentots.' The missions held thanksgiving services and some Khoikhoi lost no time in approaching the government for grants of land. The governor refused these applications on the grounds that they were made for 'the whole Hottentot population'. Land tenure at the Cape was based on individual ownership; therefore the Khoikhoi were advised to apply as individuals and not assert their land rights as a group.

The news of Ordinance 50 took much longer to reach most Khoikhoi on the farms. In early 1829 a letter to the *South African Commercial Advertiser* – the newspaper which campaigned successfully for a free press – claimed that few Khoikhoi in the interior were aware of their new rights, which ought to be explained to them individually. This letter was unusual. Most of the correspondents opposed Ordinance 50 and demanded that the government restore the pass system or enact a vagrancy law. Preventing such a law, which would reduce their hard-won freedoms, was an important concern of the Khoikhoi and their friends from this time on.

In 1829 Andries Stockenström, who

No. 50.

G.  R.

(Signed)   RICH. BOURKE.

ORDINANCE

Of His Honor the Lieutenant-Governor in Council,

For improving the Condition of Hottentots and other free Persons of colour at the Cape of Good Hope, and for consolidating and amending the Laws affecting those Persons.

WHEREAS certain Laws relating to and affecting the Hottentots and other free Persons of colour, lawfully residing in this Colony, require to be consolidated, amended, or repealed, and certain obnoxious usages and customs, which are injurious to those Persons, require to be declared illegal and discontinued: Be it therefore enacted, by His Honor the Lieutenant-Governor in Council, That from and after the passing of this Ordinance, the Proclamations of the 16th day of July, 1787, 9th day of May, 1803,—1st day of November, 1809,—23d day of April, 1812,—9th day of July, 1819,—and 23d day of May, 1823, shall be, and the same are hereby repealed: Provided always, that nothing herein contained shall extend to affect or annul any Contracts or Indentures entered into prior to the passing of this Ordinance, by virtue of the Proclamations aforesaid, nor to release the Master or Employer of any contracted Servant or Apprentice from any of the Provisions of those Proclamations relating to the Treatment, Payment, Food, Clothing, and Instruction of the said Servants and Apprentices, nor from any Fines and Penalties which may be imposed on any such Master or Employer for the breach thereof.

Repeal of former Laws.

Except as to existing Contracts.

II. And whereas by usage and custom of this Colony, Hottentots and other free Persons of colour have been subjected to certain restraints as to their residence, mode of life, and employment, and to certain compulsory services to which others of His Majesty's Subjects are not liable: Be it therefore enacted, that from and after the passing of this Ordinance, no Hottentot or other free Person of colour, lawfully residing in this Colony, shall be subject to any compulsory service to which other of His Majesty's Subjects therein are not liable, nor to any hindrance, molestation, fine, imprisonment, or punishment of any kind whatsoever, under the pretence that such Person has been guilty of vagrancy or any other offence, unless after trial in due course of Law;—any custom or usage to the contrary in any wise notwithstanding.

Hottentots and other free Persons of colour not to be molested or punished except after trial.

had become the Commissioner-General of the eastern districts of the Cape, persuaded the government to make land available to certain Khoikhoi and Bastaards in a region from which the Xhosa chief Maqoma and his people had been expelled. They were to form a buffer, to protect the colony from a revenge attack. In the words of the historian, Tony Kirk:

> The Cape authorities founded the Kat River Settlement in 1829 as a military barrier between white farmers and the Xhosa chiefdoms on the eastern Cape frontier. Lying along the headwaters of the Kat River, it comprised 640 allotments capable of irrigation, each with grazing commons attached. The average size of each allotment (known by the Dutch term *erf*) was slightly over six acres. Commonage varied from two to five hundred acres. The Settlement's boundaries also included large tracts of

Figure 63 (previous page). Ordinance 50 of 1828 made 'Hottentots and other free Persons of colour' equal with the colonists before the law. The expression 'other free Persons of colour' meant that those called 'Bushmen', 'Bastaards', or 'free blacks' were included. Slaves only acquired equal rights in 1838, four years after slavery was abolished at the Cape. 'G. R.' stands for George Rex (King George IV of Britain). Richard Bourke was the Lieutenant-Governor.

Figure 64. This party, comfortably outspanned for the night, is an example of the new mobility of the Khoikhoi after Ordinance 50. By the mid-1800s, as C.D. Bell's painting shows colonial Khoikhoi wore the same (often cast-off) clothing as the colonists. They acquired colonial goods as wages 'in kind', or through buying what they could afford, for example the fiddle, drum and wagon shown here.

Figure 65. Kat River Settlement. The Kat River settlers were recovering from a devastating frontier war (the 'sixth', of 1834–5) when Henry Butler made this drawing.

land unsuitable for either grazing or cultivation. Occupancy was reserved exclusively for coloured people.

Despite the dangers, many Khoikhoi seized the chance to acquire land and independence. Stockenström reserved the right to admit or reject the applicants. A missionary sympathised that 'their sufferings will be great in … the depth of a cold and severe winter', on an undeveloped site, but those who were eligible on account of past service in the Cape Regiment and their relative wealth in stock were not put off. In the early years of the Kat River Settlement many visitors, who knew no more of the Khoikhoi than the old stereotype concerning their 'indolence', expressed amazement at the

industry and good order which they found there. There are many detailed accounts of their impressions. Other colonists distrusted the loyalty of the Khoikhoi settlers and resented the fact that they were independent and thus no longer available as labourers.

In 1834 the colonists reacted to the emancipation of the slaves with even louder demands for a vagrancy law. An ordinance was drafted, making it possible for anyone to be picked up and prosecuted for vagrancy. Reacting to this ordinance, the Kat River Khoikhoi spoke their hearts on the meaning of the freedoms they had gained as a result of Ordinance 50 and the Settlement. In a memorable phrase, Andries Stoffels remarked:

'The 50 Ordinance came out, then did we first taste freedom … that other men eat so sweet … and now that it is mingled with Water & Ground it is 20 times sweeter than forced labour'. Other speakers made the point that there could be 'no midway between slavery and freedom'; if they could be arrested as vagrants, they would again be no different from slaves. At Theopolis, a mission institution in Albany district where many of the Kat River people formerly lived, Platje Jonker put the prospect bluntly: 'I fear a vagrant is something like a dog, you may knock him on the head and no notice will be taken of it.'

These Khoikhoi were just some of many who spoke with eloquence and feeling, and whose words were recorded by their own 'scribes'. 'It forms a new

Figure 66. 'Romance and Reality, or Hottentots as they are said to be and are.'
This caricature (or likeness of anything so distorted as to appear ridiculous) is one of a series by Frederick I'ons which reflected settler opinion about certain policies which had been introduced. The only individual in the picture who is named is 'J. Phillip' – Dr John Philip of the London Missionary Society. Philip's book, Researches in Southern Africa, *which argued that the Khoikhoi should have equal rights and treatment with other free persons at the Cape, had recently appeared (in 1828). Many colonists resented the book, and the so-called 'Hottentot Emancipation' (Ordinance 50) of the same year. In England, too, many people were against reforms which gave more rights to 'lower' classes and emancipated the slaves.*
Was the purpose of the cartoon only to amuse, or did the picture have another purpose – for example, to influence opinion and turn the public away from supporting the reforms which Dr Philip wanted?

Figure 67. In 1884 the artist for The South African Illustrated News produced a series featuring 'the types of natives' found at the Cape. This example (left) was described as follows: 'This admirable sketch by Schröder is of a well-known herd at De Aar. 'Piet' is typical of his class, and we have a very good idea conveyed to us of the barren Karoo, which after all is such an admirable sheep country.' Piet's dress and condition contrast with the romanticised shepherd by G. F. Angas (right).

era in the politics of the colony, the Hottentots as a nation petitioning for their Civil Rights,' one of the missionaries observed. When the vagrancy draft ordinance was referred to London, it was disallowed, but the issue was far from settled. Later measures tipped the balance between masters and servants to the advantage of the masters, while conditions at Kat River and Theopolis became more stressful. Both settlements were exposed to fearful loss and danger during the sixth (1834–5) and seventh (1846) frontier wars. Those of the brave and forceful speakers of 1834 who survived until the 1850s watched as yet another war destroyed these bases for

Khoikhoi independence.

Ordinance 50 has been described both as a 'great injury to masters' and as a 'great act of emancipation', depending on the writer's point of view. We may note that, though it clarified the right of 'Hottentots and other free persons of colour' (not slaves) to land, it did not put land within their reach. As William Boyce, a Wesleyan missionary said, the colonial government did only 'half' of what it should have done: 'The Hottentots had only one-half of their wrongs redressed; they were restored to liberty and freedom of action, but they were not placed in the possession of land or other property, as some compensation for the whole colony and the numerous flocks taken from their ancestors.'

Stockenström's allocation to the Khoikhoi of a region beyond the settled districts was a familiar mix of concern for their 'betterment' and for the Colony's own defence. For the vast majority of Khoikhoi, their greatest gain from Ordinance 50 was their new freedom to move about as they wished. Those with a few animals could squat on vacant (Crown or government) land, or on the grazing places of the farmers if they had friends among their Khoikhoi herdsmen. Some moved to villages and towns. Their mobility upset their former masters, so they had to remain constantly on the watch for renewed restrictions on their freedom. The memory of passes, indenture (*inboek*) and their former 'slavery', as they had felt it, remained keen.

No easy road

After Ordinance 50 and the freeing of the slaves, at the end of four years of 'apprenticeship' (1834–8), laws were introduced which made life difficult for the already marginalised sections of Cape society.

An 1836 ordinance gave villages and towns the power to elect municipal boards which, though not subject to a colour bar, became exclusively white. These boards forced newly mobile 'coloured' workers, who were too poor to rent or purchase dwellings on the same basis as white townspeople, to rent sites in municipal 'locations' on the fringes of towns. With no effort by central government to oversee their management, these ghettos grew up without amenities (piped water, municipal sanita-

tion) even where their residents paid rates into a town's revenue account.

The Masters and Servants Ordinance of 1841 followed a directive by the British Colonial Office to the effect that the former slave colonies should enact legislation to replace the old slave codes. Since Ordinance 50 applied to 'Hottentots and other free persons of colour', it would have been possible to include freed slaves under the existing law. However, it was decided to write a new 'colour-blind' law which would apply to servants in the broadest sense. The 1828 ordinance was rewritten and expanded. One clause increased the benefits for sick and injured workers but, for the most part, clauses were tightened up to better suit employers. As no changes to Ordinance 50 could be introduced without the sanction of the British government, the drafters were careful not to overstep the likely limits of their tolerance. At this point the histories of the San, Khoikhoi and former slaves began to converge, and the term 'coloured people' was sometimes used in contemporary records.

The 1850s: a turning point

Many things changed in the 1850s. John Philip and James Read, who had devoted their lives to representing Khoikhoi interests as they saw them, died in the early 1850s. The humanitarian movement to which they had appealed was losing its capacity and will to intervene. Critics complained, as before, that labour was locked up in mission stations. They objected to the fact that missionaries carried out the functions of magistrates, such as discipline and punishment.

A new constitution (1853) introduced a system of representative government at the Cape. This had been opposed by 'the articulate Coloured opinion of the day'. Petitioners at the Kat River Settlement protested that 'an African Parliament will be detrimental to the interests of Her Majesty's aboriginal subjects' but the movement towards self-rule could not be checked. The historian Stanley Trapido has described the political manoeuvring which resulted in a low franchise qualification. A number of 'coloured' men were enfranchised when occupiers of property to the value of £25 were given the vote. For example, a hundred men at Mamre, a Moravian mission in the western Cape, qualified. But the 'coloured' voters were spread out across the country and so were unable to wield much political influence.

An immediate result of the new system of government was a sharp rise in expenditure and in the Colony's deficit. One remedy was the selling off, or else the leasing at economic rates, of Crown land; that is, land at the disposal of the government. This affected those still squatting near towns, as well as marginalised stock-owners who relied on Crown lands for pasturage.

In 1856 the Legislative Council amended the 1841 Masters and Servants Ordinance to meet the wishes of employers who wanted longer contracts, child indenture, and stiffer punishment. One reason why the farmers pressed for strong labour controls was the passing of the Burgher Force Bill in the previous year (8 June 1855). This Act, which overhauled the old commando system, would result in periods away from home and landowners saw the existing controls as too weak to safeguard their homes and families in their absence.

Under the Burgher Force Bill, veldcornets were required to prepare lists 'of all the male residents … between the ages of 20 and 50 years'. 'Coloured' men were eligible for conscription, but their inclusion in the 'burgher force' gave rise to hostile demonstrations in several districts.

Also on 8 June, an Act creating divisional councils came into force. Voters on the parliamentary roll elected councillors who managed district affairs such as roads, pounds, schools, the alienation of public lands, licences and so forth. This measure meant that white inhabitants had gained control of both central and local (municipal and district) governments.

While these events were taking place, a cataclysm overtook the Kat River Settlement and other regions of the Cape.

'Mlanjeni's War' and the Khoikhoi Rebellion of 1850–3

After Ordinance 50 the colonial elite (merchants and the wealthier farmers, particularly) became more powerful because of the municipal boards and the strengthening of controls by employers over their servants. This made the Khoikhoi more aware of their lack of power. At this point, 'Khoikhoi' refers to the descendants of the Cape herders, and not 'herders' as such; by the mid-1800s amalgamation of the Khoikhoi and former slaves had not occurred to the extent where they can jointly be called 'the coloured people', although the term was sometimes used. The Khoikhoi felt persecuted because of the ongoing threat of anti-squatting and vagrancy laws, their inability to acquire land or gain extensions to crowded missions, the money they lost when their cattle were impounded, the onrush of representative government which they opposed, and other developments. The historian Clifton Crais describes how, late in 1850, word began to spread among the people of Kat River and the labourers on eastern Cape farms that they should band together to overthrow their new oppressors. Since the war of independence against the Dutch farmers (of 1799–1803), many of the frontier Boers had left on their 'Great Trek'. By 1850, certain of the British settlers had become the persons most determined to control labour and monopolise access to land.

Willem Uithaalder of Kat River became the leader of those Khoikhoi settlers who decided to rebel. Crais has used archival sources which reveal how the 'fateful message' of rebellion spread, for example, from Uithaalder to farmworkers via his brother-in-law Koetgan (an ex-slave known also as Africa April). Koetgan swore that 'before he would again become' a slave 'it would cost blood'. What followed in 1851 has been called by Crais 'the most widespread conflict the Cape Colony would see for a full century' – referring to South Africa's recent history. Large numbers, estimated at above three-quarters, of farm servants in the border districts rebelled, as did the residents of two eastern missions (Theopolis and Shiloh) and perhaps a quarter of the Kat River men. Missionaries living in the settlement feared the outcome and warned the rebels not to proceed, but Uithaalder told them:

> Sir, you [W. R. Thomson] and Mr Read were both young when you came among us, and you are now both old, and klein Mynheer (young Mr Read) had no beard when he came to Kat River, and he is now getting advanced in years, and yet these oppressions won't cease. The Missionaries have for years written, and their writings won't help. We are now going to stand up for our own affairs. We shall show the settlers that we too are men.

The rebellion of the Khoikhoi is sometimes invisible in accounts of the 'eighth frontier war', which is also known as 'Mlanjeni's War' because of the influence of the Xhosa prophet Mlanjeni, who was blamed for the Xhosa attack on the colony on Christmas Day, 1850. Their part in the conflict has been described by Crais. The colonists were afraid that Khoikhoi and ex-slaves would rise throughout the colony. This did not happen, and the Khoikhoi–Xhosa allies on the eastern frontier were defeated in the end.

The price of their rebellion was very high. Many rebels were killed and some of the survivors, including Koetgan, were tried for treason. Andries Botha, a Kat River field cornet who was renowned for faithful service to the colony, received the death sentence but was released. Kat River was no longer reserved for exclusive occupation by people of colour. The *erven* of the rebels were confiscated as were those of persons who were later proved to have taken no part in the rebellion. White colonists bought up this land. The Moravian mission, Shiloh, was spared, but the government revoked the Theopolis lands, forcing it to close. Some serving members of the Cape Mounted Riflemen (formerly the Cape Regiment) had defected to the rebels, and so the

Figure 68. 'Kat River veldkornet Andries Botha, a war hero who, in his old age, was sentenced to death as a rebel.' (Alf Wannenburgh)

CMR virtually ceased enlisting Khoikhoi recruits. When it disbanded in 1870 it had just ten men who were not white.

The Kat River experiment had been suspect in the minds of many colonists and the rebellion seemed to confirm their fears. This took no account of the many grievances which, for a start, included delays in issuing title-deeds to the plot holders and their losses (and loyal service) in two previous frontier wars. Undoubtedly it counted against the Kat River people that the settlement had been a base from which they could express their own sense of history and of politics.

The Khoikhoi people's quest for status as equals in the land of their birth had largely failed, as had their search for independence on the fringes of the colony. Across the middle Orange, Griqua self-rule was infringed as a result of Britain's recognition of the Boer statelet, the Orange River Sovereignty. In 1861 the Philippolis Griqua made a difficult and costly trek across the Drakensberg to 'Nomansland' (later East Griqualand). This and other stories which concern the courage and perseverance of Khoikhoi and Bastaards, who struggled to achieve autonomy through thick and thin, may be read in *Forgotten Frontiersmen* by Alf Wannenburgh.

Inside the Cape Colony, the setbacks of the 1850s made it appear that resistance had come to an end, though many colonists were still easily alarmed by any hint that the Khoikhoi might rebel again.

Khoikhoi resistance after their 'emancipation'

'The notion that "Coloureds" were politically passive during the period between emancipation and the 1890s is a long standing myth', John Marincowitz has declared. This historian points out that though poor whites had access to colonial elites, which poor blacks lacked, the latter were not without resource: many avoided wage labour by squatting on public (unappropriated) lands. In 1851 an ordinance 'To Prevent the Practice of Settling or Squatting upon Government Lands' was introduced – but the threat that resentful workers in the western Cape would join the eastern rebels (see 'Mlanjeni's War') raised such alarm that this ordinance had to be scrapped.

The 1860s and 1870s were times of turmoil among the Gariep, on the Cape's north-west frontier. White farmers moved onto lands which appeared empty but which had, in fact, long been used

Figure 69. Members of the Griqua Commission to Nomansland in 1860. From left to right: Abraham le Fleur, Adam 'Muis' Kok, Johannes Ullbricht, Frederick Werner, John de Bruin, Dirk Swartz. Abraham le Fleur, who was born at Uitenhage, became an important Griqua politician and was the father of Andrew Abraham Stockenström le Fleur (see fig. 73 and p. 122).

Figure 70. 'Ian Tzatzoe, Andries Stoffels, the Revd Dr Philip & Revd Messrs Read Senr & Junr giving Evidence before the Committee of the House of Commons.' The party spent some months in England and their testimony to the Select Committee on Aborigines (1836) appears in a lengthy report. Tzatzoe (or Tshatshu) was a Xhosa, Stoffels a Gonaqua Khoikhoi, Philip a Scot, Read (sen.) English-born and Read (jun.) the son of Read and his Khoikhoi wife, Elizabeth Valentyn.

Figure 71. Printing presses were prized by the missionaries for producing their own teaching materials which, for the most part, were of a religious nature. As seen here, young mission residents were trained as printers.

for seasonal grazing by a branch of the Khoikhoi known as Korana. Faced with the loss of pastures and water essential to survival in an arid region, the Korana – who were given to frequent cattle raids among themselves – began to raid the farmers' herds. Two wars, which devastated the Korana, ensued in 1869 and 1878–9. The historian Teresa Strauss has characterised the lifestyle of the Korana as 'almost an anachronism'. These wars, too, had more the character of early episodes of Khoikhoi resistance than of contemporary struggles by the colonial Khoikhoi.

Andrew Abraham Stockenström le Fleur represents another strand in the web of Khoi challenges to colonial rule. The son of a leading Griqua politician, and husband to the daughter of Adam 'Muis' Kok, regarded as Adam Kok III's heir, Le Fleur aspired to be the Griqua captain and vigorously asserted their land claims. After several incidents he was arrested and, in April 1898, imprisoned for sedition. After his release in

1903, he promoted self-help and settlement schemes among his followers. In Christopher Saunders' words, Le Fleur came to feel that 'Griquas and other "Coloureds" should live and develop in separate communities'. Later he disseminated his ideas through the Griqua Independent Church and a newspaper which he founded.

Khoikhoi in the late 1800s

The possibility of rising on the social scale and gaining acceptance by means of education and 'respectable' trades appeared less likely than it had done when the mission enterprise was young and optimistic. When Andries Stoffels testified before the British House of Commons' Select Committee on Aborigines in 1836, he answered questions as follows:

> Has the character and condition of the Hottentots improved since the missionaries came among them?
>
> Yes.
>
> In what respects have their character

Figure 72. These drawings by an artist identified simply as 'I. W.' are based on earlier caricatures by Charles D. Bell. Images were often 'recycled' in this way and thus remained in circulation.

and condition improved?

The young people can now read and write, and we all wear clothes; many of us have learnt trades, and are altogether better men.

Have they got any knowledge of agriculture?

We have ploughing, wagonmakers, and shoemakers, and other tradesmen amongst us; we can make all those things except a watch and a coach.

There was still reason to expect continued progress in this direction at the time. However, the historian Jane Sales explains how in the 1840s policy that government schools be open to all children was undermined, and 'coloured'

children for the most part were confined to separate, mission schools. Some Khoikhoi set up as artisans or migrated as labourers to the towns. The Moravians, for example, established urban institutions to retain connections with church members who left the rural institutions. Out of centres such as these, small numbers of teachers and others with a formal education began to emerge.

Old stereotypes of the Khoikhoi were kept alive. Andrew Geddes Bain's performance poem titled 'Kaatje Kekkelbek', which appeared in 1838 and mocked the Khoikhoi of the Kat River Settlement, always found a ready audience:

Figure 73. Andrew Abraham Stockenström Le Fleur with his followers at Kokstad jail in 1898, when he was sentenced to 14 years' imprisonment with hard labour for attempting to wage war. Le Fleur founded the Griqua Reformation Movement which aimed to unite the coloured people. He was granted early release from his prison sentence and returned to active politics.

My name is Kaatje Kekkelbek
I kom van Kat Rivier
Dere is van water geen gebrek
Maar scarce van wyn en beer.
Myn a.b.c. at Philip's school
I learnt ein kleene bietjie
and left, with wisdom just as full
As gekke tante Meitjie.

Saartje Baartman's steatopygous figure had become a cliché of the cartoonist's art. In 1877 a literary journal, *The Cape Monthly Magazine*, amused its readers with a disreputable piece titled 'The Diary of an Idle Hottentot' by an anonymous writer who used the name 'Adonis Jager'. Many such examples can be found. Referring to jokes and other aspects of popular culture, historian Mohammed Adhikari shows how the 'association of illegitimacy, savagery and marginality coalesce in the stereotyping of coloured people in the popular mind.'

Under these conditions, did a sense of nationhood or nationalism develop among erstwhile Cape herders? This is an important question for researchers of the patchy archive with respect to the Khoikhoi. Trapido has said that, out of the agitations against a vagrancy law in 1834, a conviction emerged among the Khoikhoi's 'leading men that a Hottentot nation existed'. He adds that, ' "Hottentot" nationalism was a social phenomenon of some complexity which was to have far-reaching consequences' in certain regards. A scholar of nationalism, Benedict Anderson, observes that 'the word "nationalism" … did not occur … in many standard nineteenth century lexicons' and when 'nation' was used (as it often was by people commenting on the Khoikhoi, and by the Khoikhoi about themselves) it may have meant 'no more

than "societies" or "states" '. The story of the Le Fleur family, in Wannenburgh's book, is called 'Nation becomes a faith'. The idea of nationalism may prove to be a rich vein of inquiry for historians to pursue.

Historians of the 1800s have to take account of the many forces which were then at work: imperialism, new concepts of statehood, and, above all, capitalism and liberalism which, together and separately, entailed free labour, free trade, industrialisation, secure rights of private property and the rule of law. In colonial settings there was often violent opposition to principles promoted by the mother country. The notion of free labour is a prime example: former slave colonies around the world demanded new forms of unfree labour. Colonial powers saw no option but to give in to them when it was clear that home manufacture and consumption would decline if the plantations lacked plentiful, cheap labour on which production relied. In colonies of settlement such as the Cape, the home government often took the line of least resistance, and allowed repressive measures which the colonists insisted that they needed to enact.

In southern Africa, there are many examples of unfree labour in the late 1800s and beyond. Everywhere – in the old provinces of Natal, Orange Free State, and Transvaal – the subordination of Africans to farm labour or to 'independence' in reserves was following the patterns first tried out and forced upon the Cape herders and hunters, the Khoikhoi and San.

The modern period:
the Namaqualand reserves

9

By the end of the 1800s little remained of the pastoralist lifestyle of the Khoikhoi. Colonial expansion had put unprecedented pressure on available land. The government usually supported the settlers' land claims and rights at the expense of the indigenous population. The late 1800s were accompanied by increased demand for wage-labour, and many people took the new opportunities offered to them and went to work in the urban and mining centres.

However, in some parts of the Cape Colony descendants of the Khoikhoi had managed to retain their rights to the land. They had done so by recognising that missionaries could offer some protection from encroaching Boers and Bastaards (or Basters, as they came to be called). There are even some reports of Namaqualand Khoikhoi travelling all the way to the Cape in search of missionaries. By 1900 numerous mission stations had been established. The mission stations were recognised by the government of the Cape Colony by way of 'tickets of occupation' which gave the indigenous population some guarantee of permanent access to the land around such settlements.

A system of government developed in many of these mission stations, whereby

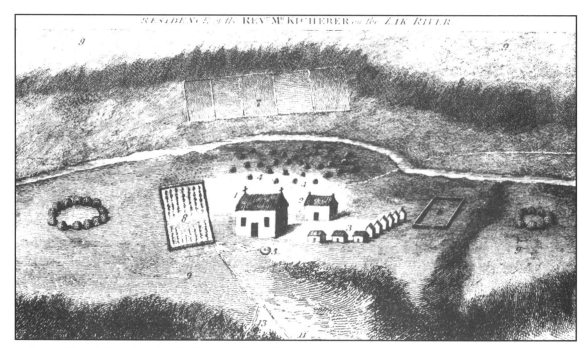

Figure 74. Zak River Mission Station, Northern Cape, c. 1804.

a *raad* (council) of elected or appointed members of the community, chaired by the missionary, was established. In order to relieve the missionaries of secular administrative duties and to grant a measure of local autonomy to the population, the Mission Stations and Communal Reserves Act (No. 29 of 1909) provided for the separation of secular and church administration, by replacing the councils with Advisory or Management Boards.

These areas became known as 'reserves', 'coloured reserves' or 'coloured rural areas', and over twenty such reserves have continued to this day. Many of them are relatively small, being no larger than adjacent white-owned farms, but they continue to provide some form of security to their several thousand inhabitants. However, a few reserves, notably those in Namaqualand, are much larger. The five Namaqualand

reserves (Richtersveld, Steinkopf, Leliefontein, Concordia and Komaggas) are amongst the six largest in the country and have a total area of over 1,5 million hectares. They are also located in what was until very recently the most isolated part of South Africa. It is in these reserves that we find farmers with significant herds of sheep and goats moving in a semi-nomadic pattern on communal land. It is also here that we have an opportunity to observe possible continuities with the Khoikhoi past.

By looking at the way in which people have lived on these Namaqualand reserves since the mid-1900s, we hope to show to what extent people have adapted to changing circumstances and have tried to retain some semblance of their independence in the face of continuing encroachment on their land, administrative changes, the rise of large towns and the intervention of outsiders.

Figure 75. The Mission Settlement at Khuboes around the turn of the century.

The Namaqualand reserves

Settler expansion from the Cape meant that the few remaining indigenous populations found themselves in the most remote, isolated and arid regions of the country.

With a poorly distributed annual rainfall of less than 150 mm, Namaqualand remains the most sparsely populated region in South Africa. There is just over one person per square kilometre. The first tarred road was constructed in the late 1960s, and the nearest rail link is still at Bitterfontein, some 180 km from Springbok. The low rainfall and severe droughts make the area only marginally suited to sedentary farming. But rich copper deposits at O'okiep and Nababeep, vast diamond deposits at the mouth of the Orange River and crayfish along the coast, all provided the stimulus for significant economic activity in the region. It is against this background that

the reserve populations have managed to survive to the present time, in spite of outside pressures.

Outsiders visiting the reserves today will notice the herds of sheep and goats, each with its own herdsman, and the *matjieshuise* still to be found in some villages. But such apparent remains of an ancient past are deceptive. In all spheres, from economic activity to the profiles of the reserve populations, major changes have occurred.

In each of the reserves permanent villages have been established. Today they provide all the basic facilities associated with village settlement – schools, shops, churches, clinics and post offices. But when the missionaries initially arrived, the church was the only attraction of village settlement. In general, schools were only established later. Not surprisingly, the missionaries initially had difficulty keeping in touch with the scattered nomadic populations. An elderly informant once recalled an image of the missionary on horseback 'herding' his congregation to church on Sundays – and making full use of his whip as a means of persuasion.

Reserve	Area in hectares	Population estimate
Richtersveld	513 919	3 200
Steinkopf	329 301	6 500
Leliefontein	192 791	5 500
Komaggas	62 603	3 400
Concordia	63 383	4 600

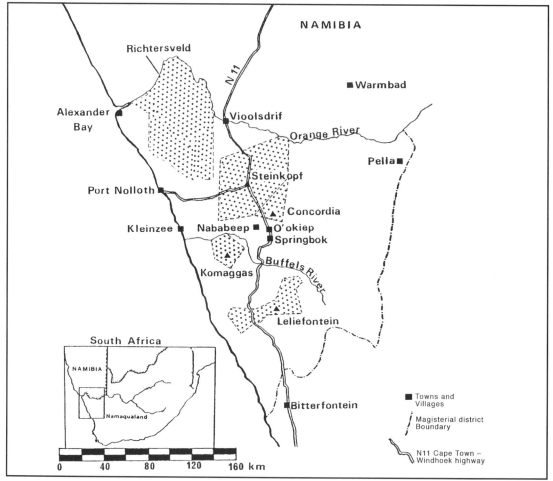

Figure 76. The Namaqualand Reserves in 1957.

Although they tried to induce people to settle in close proximity to the mission stations by encouraging the cultivation of irrigated vegetable gardens and dry wheat fields, there are several reports of locals returning to a nomadic existence during gaps in the missionary presence.

However, grazing in the immediate vicinity of the mission stations quickly became depleted. The populations then established separate outposts, either smaller permanent settlements or very mobile stock-posts, at some distance from the villages. Stock-posts have become an integral part of stock farming in the reserves. They permit the herds of sheep and goats to maintain maximum mobility, without needing to return to the village every evening. Until the late 1950s it was still possible for farmers to live at their stock-posts. But with the establishment of schools and an increasing dependence on shops (associated with the move away from a subsistence lifestyle), it became increasingly difficult for farmers and their families to live permanently with their herds. The pattern of permanent village settlement that resulted meant that farmers required the constant attendance of a herdsman to

Figure 77. Matjieshuis *alongside conventional present-day house, Leliefontein, Namaqualand, 1991.*

look after their herds.

At the same time there was increasing involvement by the reserve population in wage-labour in the region. There was work on the mines, on white-owned farms and, to a lesser extent, in the fishing industry. The fact that the populations in the reserves have remained almost constant since the 1950s indicates that there has been a very high rate of permanent out-migration. Some reserve-dwellers have moved out of the reserves with their families to towns in the area, but many families also moved out of the Namaqualand region and settled in the larger centres, including Cape Town, where they were absorbed into the coloured population.

At first, the district magistrates controlled the administration of the Management Boards, but in the 1950s they were placed under the control of the Department of Coloured Affairs (subsequently the Administration of Coloured Affairs and then the House of Representatives). The structure of the boards, however, remained the same throughout this period. They consisted of elected or appointed members of the community, but were ultimately under the control of an outside chairman (missionary, magistrate or bureaucratic 'superintendent'). But it would be wrong to view them, even during the early missionary phase, as extensions of the traditional tribal councils, even though there was local representation and the use of terms such as *kaptein* and *korporaal* for certain members.

During the early period the *rade*, or boards, were primarily concerned with day-to-day matters relating to the maintenance of order, settlement of disputes, and the granting of residence and grazing

Race classification in South Africa

South African society has, since the arrival of the first settlers, been characterised by racial stratification. Status or position in society has been associated with physical features such as skin colour.

The boundaries between these social categories, especially in the case of Namaqualand, were neither clear nor fixed. There was no absolute line between light- and dark-skinned people; there was extensive social interaction and intermarriage between people of different racial backgrounds; and not all whites were wealthy, or blacks poor.

In 1950 the apartheid government tried to make these boundaries more rigid by introducing a system of racial classification. The Population Registration Act (No. 30 of 1950) allocated every South African to one of three basic categories: 'White', 'Native' and 'Coloured'. A 'Native' was defined as 'a member of any aboriginal race or tribe of Africa', and therefore included Bushmen and Hottentots. In the early 1950s many descendants of the Khoikhoi, including many people in the northern Richtersveld, were classified as 'Natives', but this categorisation was later changed to 'Coloured'. Most descendants of the Khoikhoi were considered to be of 'mixed' descent and therefore not classified as 'Natives', but were assigned to the 'Coloured Group' instead. The 'Coloured' category was essentially a miscellaneous category for anyone who was 'not a white person or a native'.

Most of the people in permanent populations of the reserves were classified as 'Coloured', simply because they were resident in Coloured Reserves. And those who left the reserves to settle permanently in towns and cities elsewhere were incorporated into the 'Coloured' populations there. Before the introduction of the Population Registration Act many lighter-skinned people entering the cities and large towns from the Namaqualand reserves were able to 'pass for white' and were accepted into this upper stratum of urban society. The 1950 legislation made this difficult, but some individuals, as late as the 1970s, were still able to obtain formal 'reclassification' if they could show that they had been accepted as 'Whites' in the urban areas.

rights. By the 1950s, however, their function had changed considerably and they focused on issues of 'development', such as town planning, provision of services, and the erection of fences, wind-pumps and reservoirs.

One key area of concern for the *rade* throughout has been the issue of control over residence and grazing rights in the reserve areas – a concern which has continued into the present period.

The mission stations, like the traditional tribal areas before them, were less concerned with the exact boundaries of their domain than with the focal centres, such as water-holes or mission stations, within them. In their early stages the missions consisted of a central station surrounded by 'zones of occupation', but these were gradually replaced by 'tickets of occupation' which did define exact boundaries. In general, these boundaries were much smaller than the original zones of occupation.

Once formal recognition of control over an area of land had been obtained, and in response to ever-increasing pressures on land, a system of community organisation developed whereby *burgerskap* (citizenship) was granted to members of the reserve community. This system, introduced by the missionaries, guaranteed access to mission reserve land to all those who achieved *burgerskap*. Only *burgers* were eligible to serve on the *raad* and this enabled the burgers to control outsiders' access.

It would also be incorrect to assume that the current residents of the reserves are all direct descendants of the Khoikhoi. After 1850 significant numbers of skilled and semi-skilled workers from other countries entered Namaqualand in response to work opportunities offered by the opening of the copper mines and the discovery of valuable fishing resources. Among these were tin min-

ers from Cornwall and fishermen from St Helena. There were also individual prospectors and even some survivors of shipwrecks from earlier times who decided to settle in the area. Many of them took wives and thus became absorbed into the Khoikhoi population, as shown by names such as Philips, Thomas and Flagg. But there was also the ongoing process of intermarriage between European (primarily Dutch) settler farmers and Khoikhoi women. The descendants of such 'mixed' unions rapidly became known as Basters (or Bastaards) and were the first group of trekboers (pioneer farmers) to move into Namaqualand from the south. By the 1860s it was reported that almost all of the inhabitants of Komaggas and Concordia were Bastaards, and by the 1950s it was widely accepted that there were 'hardly any pure Hottentots left in Namaqualand'.

All of this serves to show the massive cultural, social and genetic interrelationship between the various populations in

Burgers, bywoners and vreemdelinge

The reserve areas, and the mission stations before them, provided residence, grazing and even arable land for a wide range of people. But not all people resident in the reserves were accorded full status as *burgers* or citizens.

Full *burgers* were entitled to use the communal grazing land, they were allocated cultivable lands where available, and they could participate in elections and stand for office on the *raad*. *Burgers* were also obliged to pay an annual tax as set by the *raad*. The exercise of these rights was optional. Many *burgers* left the reserves, and unless they continued

to pay taxes, forfeited their citizenship rights.

But there were two other categories of residents who were not regarded as *burgers*. There were *vreemdelinge* (outsiders), such as the missionaries themselves, schoolteachers, traders and some farmers who were given temporary residence rights and even rights to grazing or cultivable land, by the *raad*. They were not, however, considered part of the reserve community even though many of them had lived in the reserves for many years and some had married locals.

There was also the category of *bywoners* (co-residents). Many of these had long associations with the reserves, but were not granted full citizenship rights. They were, instead, incorporated into the reserve community because of their relationships with individual *burgers*, generally as herdsmen or sharecroppers on cultivable fields. Consequently they were also often referred to as *bediendes* (servants).

The similarities between the *vreemdelinge* of the present in the reserves and the outsiders who were given temporary rights to grazing in Khoikhoi tribal areas (see p. 39), and between *bywoners* and servants or dependants (see pp 31–2), are quite striking. *Vreemdelinge* and outsiders were both seen as temporary sojourners: outsiders were given grazing rights in return for a tribute or a gift, while *vreemdelinge* were given access to land or residence rights either in return for services rendered to the community or for a set charge. Servants or dependants and *bywoners* were incorporated into the community only as dependants or clients with intimate links to full members of the tribe or citizens of the reserve.

But such similarities do not necessarily show any direct continuity from the past. The patterns of today may not have developed out of earlier forms. In fact, it is significant to note that in the Richtersveld, where relative isolation has to some extent shielded the local population from outside influences, the institutions of *vreemdeling* and *bywoner* have not evolved. All that we can conclude, therefore, is that both sets of institutions are adaptations whereby outsiders could be accommodated within either the tribal or reserve communities without threatening the rights of permanent members.

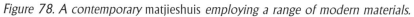

Figure 78. A contemporary matjieshuis *employing a range of modern materials.*

Racial stratification: Khoikhoi, Basters and whites

With the settlement of Europeans at the Cape came new pressure on land and a process of population displacement. The most marginalised people were forced by this to move northwards and eastwards. But such displaced people were not moving into uninhabited areas, with the result that there was a ripple effect on population pressure which was felt far across the land.

Put very simply, Khoikhoi who were not incorporated as labourers into settler society moved away from the Cape in search of grazing land. They in turn displaced San and other Khoikhoi populations, only for the process to be repeated into the most remote, inhospitable and sparsely populated areas of the Cape. The Khoikhoi were later followed by the Basters and they in turn were followed by white farmers.

Although settler society at the Cape rapidly became racially stratified, the same could not be said of the Namaqualand population. Here the boundaries between white, Baster and Khoikhoi, and between land-owners, trekboers and mission-dwellers, were fluid until the end of the 1800s. Some Khoikhoi and Basters were granted individual title to land, while many whites remained landless trekboers who used remaining Crown land or entered into *bywoner* relationships with land-owners or reserve-dwellers. Intermarriage between all the categories seems to have been the norm. But, while racial boundaries may have been fluid, the Baster children of white farmers and Khoikhoi wives had little chance of being incorporated into the upper stratum, so many left the colony and trekked northwards. As individuals it was common for them to be absorbed into the local populations, as was the case for individual whites. But after 1800 it was commonly reported that certain groups of Basters – such as the 'Rehoboth Basters' who crossed the Orange River in 1868 and settled in present-day Namibia – had imbibed the racist ideology of Cape settler society and saw themselves as separate from both white and Khoikhoi peoples and tended to marry only amongst themselves. The term 'Baster', although meaning 'half-caste', was adopted without this negative connotation, for it provided people with a name which set them apart from, and so raised their status in relation to, the Khoikhoi.

These sentiments of racial superiority were also in evidence in Namaqualand throughout the 1800s, but, given the extent of intermarriage and interdependence within the whole population, they did not result in the formation of rigid social boundaries.

By the 1890s, however, the association between race and access to land had begun to harden. For example, some tickets of occupation granted to the mission stations specified that inhabitants should be 'aborigines or bastards of aboriginal descent'. This meant that mission residents came to be seen as either 'Hottentots' or 'Basters': even whites settling there became Basters by association. At the same time individual land ownership came to be increasingly associated with being 'white' and the authorities became more and more reluctant to grant individual title to people who were not 'white'.

Namaqualand. It becomes futile to try to understand the situation in the reserves today in terms of particular cultural patterns which have continued into the present. In addition, the opening of the mines had a major impact on the reserves, on the nature of farming and on racial divisions.

Social change: farming and wage-labour

Until the late 1800s stock farming in Namaqualand had prospered, and the vegetable gardens and wheat fields had proven to be remarkably successful, given the arid climate. The mission station populations were still subsistence farmers, with very little need for cash income, although they were often required to contribute towards the missionary's salary, and they did buy certain basic consumer goods, such as coffee, sugar and clothing.

By the early 1900s the mission stations had gone into a period of decline from which they did not really begin to recover until the 1950s. Outsiders who looked for an explanation for this decline were aware that it coincided with the opening of the copper mines, but generally favoured explanations in terms of the population's 'indolent and improvident habits' and the 'communalistic' system of land tenure and social organisation. But neither explanation could account for the initial period of prosperity.

The formal demarcation of the mission stations' boundaries meant a reduction in the land available to residents. The granting of individual title to whites in the region meant that there was less Crown and other unoccupied land available. This forced numerous additional landless farmers into the mission reserves. Land-owning farmers had also responded to the markets created by the opening of the mines. They were thus less inclined to accommodate *bywoners* on their farms, so *bywoners*, too, sought refuge in the reserves.

Although many reserve dwellers did enter the wage-labour market, the mines at first had great difficulty attracting enough workers for their needs. Most people in the reserves continued to try to survive on subsistence agriculture. Their protected access to land allowed them, at least to some extent, to withstand pressures from outside. And the system of communal land tenure slowed down the process whereby some local farmers could increase their land holding and force the remainder off the land.

By 1900 most reserve residents were beginning to recognise that wage-labour on the mines did not offer a viable alternative to farming on the reserves. The copper mines had been plagued by technical problems, transport difficulties (ore or copper had to be transported to Port Nolloth) and fluctuating markets. This resulted in a very irregular demand for labour. Mine-owners were not prepared or able to support large, permanent labour forces, and retrenchments were frequent.

Wage-labourers responded by maintaining their links with the reserves, protecting the institution of *burgerskap*, and defending the system of communal land ownership. This system in operation in the reserves provided workers with some long-term security. The reserves gave them guaranteed residence and housing. Many could subsist, at least in the short term, on agricultural production. They could draw on social relationships for support in times of need. In the absence of secure jobs, unemployment benefits, housing not tied to companies, and adequate pensions, the reserves offered some insurance and independence.

This pattern has continued up to the present. Reserve residents today cannot be neatly divided into 'farmers' and 'wage-labourers'. One is seen as a supplement, rather than an alternative, to the other. Surveys of households in the reserves indicate that many households have income from both wage-labour and farming. Also, personal life histories show that very few individuals have not, at various stages of their lives, been involved in both activities.

Other aspects of social change

Missionaries offered reserve residents some protection against farmers moving onto their land. They also introduced crop cultivation and the establishment of permanent village settlements. But they obviously also had a major influence on the non-economic spheres of social life.

The most significant social consequence of the missions was the rapid conversion to Christianity – a change which has led to the loss of traditional religious beliefs. However, some traditional ritual practices survived alongside Christian ones. For example, puberty rituals, for boys and girls, survived well into the twentieth century, as did traditional marriage rituals, which were sometimes held in addition to Christian ceremonies.

The introduction of schools also had a major impact on social life, especially on indigenous language. Teachers, and many parents, recognised that children who had learnt a Khoikhoi language at home were severely disadvantaged in the Afrikaans-medium schools. Most teachers thus actively discouraged children from speaking a Khoikhoi language, and parents did little to resist this trend. The result has been that Khoikhoi languages have largely been replaced by Afrikaans and are rapidly disappearing in South Africa today. Very few young people, even in the reserve areas, retain more than a smattering of their traditional language. But in Namibia it is still the mother-tongue of most of the few thousand remaining Khoikhoi herders.

Indigenous knowledge of traditional plant use is also rapidly disappearing. This is largely due to urbanisation, a cash economy, the availability of commercial alternatives, and especially the introduction of western medicine. But Fiona Archer, an ethnobotanist who has worked extensively in the Richtersveld, emphasises that traditional plant use also came to be associated with poverty and backwardness. This has meant that people do not always admit to knowledge of indigenous plants. She was thus able to document that detailed local plant knowledge is still available. She has compiled a list of over 120 species that are still recognised as edible or medicinal plants, or can be used for a range of utilitarian purposes, including the construction of *matjieshuise*, the preparation of skins, and for making soap, tools and utensils.

Continuing land struggles
& the emergence of a Nama identity

10

Outsiders, and some of the wealthier local stock-owners in the reserves, have from time to time argued that the system of communal land tenure should be abolished. Their reasoning has been that the reserves have suffered extensive overgrazing and that this is a direct consequence of the 'free-for-all' access associated with communal grazing.

Not surprisingly, the majority of residents have resisted proposals to abolish the communal land tenure system, but the debate has caused great unhappiness and divisions in the communities.

'Communal land' and 'economic units'

The most recent episode in the battle to retain the communal land tenure system began in 1963 when the government proposed the introduction of 'economic units' in the Namaqualand reserves. This scheme entailed dividing the reserves up into a number of farms or 'economic units' which would be hired out to local farmers. Provision was made for them to be sold at a later stage.

The major concern of the residents centred on the issue of who would be fortunate enough to obtain one of these units, for it was quite clear from the outset that there were insufficient units for

The 'tragedy of the commons'

In the 1960s Garrett Hardin wrote a very influential article about communal land tenure which summarised what many people felt about the inevitability of overgrazing and soil erosion.

He argued that since communal grazing was an unregulated 'free-for-all', individual farmers would attempt to increase the size of their herds beyond the carrying capacity of the land because they could see no advantage to themselves in saving and conserving the land for future use.

There is no doubt that communal land use is associated with overgrazing. But this is not necessarily inevitable or always the case.

There is ample evidence to show that traditional communal farming is regulated by a range of formal and informal social practices. Many of these survive to the present day in areas such as the northern Richtersveld, where each farmer, or group of farmers, still adheres very much to certain set tracts of land and follows regular seasonal migration patterns. There is also a strong sense, shared by the population at large, that a farmer will not enter the 'space' around another's herd, and that if rain has fallen in a certain zone, no herd should enter until the vegetation has been able to recover for two to three weeks.

There are natural factors which used to act as a means of regulating stock numbers, particularly in Namaqualand. For example, the limited number of water-holes and the frequent droughts meant that animal numbers were not able to multiply beyond the grazing in the area. At the same time, communal grazing itself allows the farmer to make use of the available resources in the most efficient manner possible. This is perhaps one reason why many farmers in the reserves do not accept the official 'carrying capacity' estimates which have been calculated on the basis of sedentary farming experience. It also allows one to understand reported observations that many of the reserves were less denuded than adjacent, individually owned farms.

Excessive population pressure in the reserves, and not communal land tenure, is clearly responsible for the overgrazing. Consequently, many people now argue that the solution to the ongoing degradation of the land in the reserves actually lies outside, and depends on the extent to which larger stock-owners can be accommodated on their own farms and wage-labourers can attain the security of jobs, housing and pensions.

all people in the reserves. In the southern part of the Richtersveld, for example, there were 37 units, ranging in size from 3 000 to 5 000 hectares. But at least 150 households owned stock. Most stock-owners would therefore be dispossessed of their rights to grazing. This problem was even more pronounced in reserves with higher population densities.

Several objections to the scheme were raised:

- It was felt that units were not economically viable, since their size had been calculated on the basis of a carrying capacity of 500 sheep or goats, and many farmers had herds which exceeded this number.
- There was concern over the rental to be

charged and the fact that individual farmers would be responsible for maintaining the wind-pumps and fences. Many also commented that they were not willing to pay for grazing rights on land which 'had always belonged to [their] ancestors'.

- The units would restrict stock movement, and not all units had wind-pumps and reservoirs.
- The most significant objection related to how the units would be allocated, and the fact that the scheme threatened to undermine the fabric of the reserves' social organisation and the delicate relationship between farming and wage-labour.

The problem of redistribution – where the little that there is becomes concentrated in the hands of a few – seems to be a common theme of development schemes in other regions as well. Local beneficiaries tend to be those who have managed to accumulate sufficient wealth, often as traders or as better-paid workers in more secure employment, to enable them to invest in farming in the reserves.

The legislation proposed that economic units be reserved only for 'bona fide

Figure 79. Proposals to replace the communal land tenure system in the Namaqualand reserves with 'economic units' were met with considerable local opposition, as this extract from a Sunday Times *report shows.*

Oom Barnie goes where he must go

Reports and Picture by Henry Ludski

Sunday Times EXTRA   19 October 1986

Inquiry into govt plan for reserves

Oom Barnie Links, 77, has strong reservations about the new scheme and is not afraid to make his point of view known.

OOM BARNIE LINKS is an old man, gnarled and bent like a weatherbeaten tree. He has lived in Namaqualand for all of his 77 years, and is not about to let anyone push him around.

He asserts with an eloquence prompted by pride and a hint of sadness: "They must not put up fences to stop me. Oom Barnie goes where he must go …"

He is one of about 800 people whose future in the dry Leliefontein district of Namaqualand rests on a government scheme whereby land has been divided into 47 "economic" units.

He and his modest herd of goats have wandered freely about the district of Tweerivier for as long as he can remember. Now he has to deal with fences and other barriers across the veld.

"I can't do what I used to do," he explains to a commission of inquiry doing the rounds of small settlements in the district.

The commissioners are there to listen to objections and comments on the desirability of the government's scheme for the 200 000-hectare area of Leliefontein – one of five coloured "reserves" in Namaqualand. The others are Steinkopf, Richtersveld, Kommaggas and Concordia.

Until 1985, most of the 4 000-odd residents owned small herds of sheep and goats, and many had rights to patches of land on which they grew wheat.

A few years ago, the government expressed concern at the extent of overgrazing in the area and set about replacing the communal system of land tenure with that of private ownership. The area was divided into units varying in size from 1 700 to 4 800 hectares.

Residents who applied for the farms in 1984 had to have 250 head of stock or R3 000 in assets. Thirty farms have been leased out on a five-year basis, after which the applicant is given the chance to buy.

Oom Barnie, who habitually refers to himself in the third person, is bitter at the prospect of change.

"Barnie fought for this land," he says. "If Barnie can't go where he wants, the way he always has, then this is no place for him. He might as well sell his goats and leave."

Why try to abolish communal land in the reserves?

The argument for abolishing communal land in the reserves has revolved around the issue of conservation and the development of the local population. But there are also other aspects which are worth considering, for they shed valuable light on those motives which too easily remain hidden.

By the 1850s there was already opposition to the granting of communal lands to the mission stations. This came, not from outsiders, but from some of the wealthier local residents seeking opportunities for advancement. Also, white farmers adjacent to some of the reserves 'cast longing eyes' on the land in the reserves and supported a proposal for full individual ownership, recognising that many plots thus created would soon be up for sale to outsiders.

Employers of labour also saw potential benefits, to themselves, from the breaking up of the reserves. Poorer residents would lose rights to the land and this would force them into wage-labour. This change would mean, however, that the mine-owners and white farmers would have to accommodate large permanent labour forces. Consequently, the government decided to retain the communal system in the reserves (the Mission Stations and Communal Reserves Act, No. 29 of 1890), but to impose an annual tax on adult males and to take measures to prevent further sub-division of arable plots. Both these measures were intended to force poorer farmers onto the labour market.

The introduction of economic units in the 1960s was aimed at the 'development' of the reserves. But some of the motivation was at least partly due to the economic aspirations of wealthy coloured farmers who were demanding the right to own individual farm land. Opportunities to acquire land in 'white' South Africa were very limited, as a result of apartheid policies as well as the costs involved.

It is also clear that official thinking was based on the model of capital accumulation of white farmers, and did not take local notions in the reserves into account.

farmers', or persons whose livelihood derives solely from farming. But, as we have seen, most owners of large herds relied heavily on other sources of income to help them build up their stock numbers. Many wealthier members of the reserve communities (including, for example, shopkeepers, fishermen and retired teachers) were granted units, whether farming was their sole livelihood or not, and this caused additional dissatisfaction.

Eventually, in the late 1980s, members of the Leliefontein community took the case to the courts and the government was forced to withdraw the scheme, not only in Leliefontein, but also in most of the other reserves where it had been implemented.

The Richtersveld National Park

In the 1970s, while the struggle over economic units was going on, conservationists began to motivate for the establishment of a nature reserve in the northern Richtersveld.

In glossy magazines, plans for the proposed park were heralded as a great achievement for conservation. It was argued that the environment had to be protected, presumably from the local population, 'before it is lost to posterity forever'. No mention was made of the fact that the local population stood to lose at least 80 000 hectares of valuable grazing land.

Although negotiations with the *raad* were already at an advanced stage, until 1985 most residents remained unaware of these plans. The Richtersveld *raad*, like those in most other reserves, was seen by locals as an unrepresentative and autocratic instrument of the state and not in touch with the local community. But in 1989, when the park was about to be proclaimed, a local delegation acting on behalf of the Community Committee, a body established in direct opposition to the *raad*, travelled to Cape Town to apply for an interdict to prevent the signing. After this action the *raad* representatives were no longer willing to sign the contract on behalf of the local population. The signing was postponed and a series of meetings, now including the Community Committee, was scheduled.

At that stage the National Parks Board policy was that parks existed for the benefit of tourists and the protection of flora and fauna. They began to recognise, however, that local populations were a political force and that international conservation movements were increasingly acknowledging that humans were an integral part of the environment.

The people of the Richtersveld had on their side some very powerful arguments. They wanted to know why a reserve area, rather than white-owned farms, was the only place where there was still something to protect. They pointed out that people were being asked to relinquish land that had belonged to their forefathers for the past 2 000 years. And they emphasised that land was a communal resource that belonged to future generations and that no one had the right to dispose of it.

When it was recognised that no park could be viable with such local opposition, significant concessions were made and a new contract was drawn up. Provision was made for local farmers to retain grazing rights in the proposed

Figure 80. After lengthy consulation with the local population, a revised contract between the Parks Board and residents of the Richtersveld was eventually signed in July 1971. Pictured here is a Parks Board official receiving a gift to symbolise acceptance into the community at the elaborated ceremony staged to mark the occasion.

The outcome of negotiations between the National Parks Board and the Richtersveld community

As the first National Park in southern Africa to incorporate land rights for the local population, the Richtersveld case marks a significant departure from traditional conservation thinking about the role of local people in the 'environment'.

The renegotiated lease demonstrates the concessions that have had to be made to the local population.

Negotiated lease	Original proposal
• lease period of 30 years	• 99-year lease
• local access to grazing in the park retained	• all stock to be removed
• locals may collect certain plants and other resources (e.g. medicinal plants, honey)	• no rights to utilise any resources
• guaranteed employment of locals by Parks Board	• no employment guarantees

park area. A joint management committee, with half of the representatives coming from the local community, was established to run the park.

But not all the members of the community approve of the impact that the park has had, and yet again we can see how outside intervention has challenged notions of shared rights and privileged a few over others. There is, for example, some unhappiness about the way in which applicants for the Parks Board posts were selected. Also, since free access to grazing in the park area cannot be permitted, a maximum of 6 600 head of stock has been determined. But this has translated into continued access for some farmers and the total exclusion of others. In particular, farmers are concerned because in the past the park area used to provide valuable emergency grazing for additional farmers during times of severe drought.

The emergence of a Nama identity

Up to the mid-1980s people in the Namaqualand reserves were acutely aware of the derogatory connotations of terms such as 'Hottentot', 'Hotnot' and even 'Nama'. Their geographic isolation increased their marginal status in South African society, as did outsiders' descriptions of them as 'backward', 'primitive' and 'simple'.

Some, as we have seen, tried to underplay or deny their Khoikhoi links. Their Baster identity was emphasised in order to stress their close associations with whites and distance from Khoikhoi. This trend is clearly reflected in the notion of *vorentoetrouery* (marriage upwards), where some Basters selectively tried to marry people of lighter skin-colour in an attempt to *uitBaster* (breed out) Khoikhoi features.

Others were constantly reminded that they were seen as inferior to both whites and Basters. There is ample evidence to show how missionaries, administrators, teachers and employers favoured Basters and looked down on those who appeared to have close Khoikhoi links. Consequently many rejected the name 'Nama', even though they might still have spoken Nama and they could easily have claimed descent from the original Namaqua inhabitants of the area. The term *boorling* (native to the area) was acceptable to some, but many promoted the idea that they were coloureds. In this they were no doubt conscious of the fact that some of them had originally been classified as 'Native' in the 1950s.

But by the end of the 1980s these attitudes had begun to change quite dramatically. Wage-labourers on the mines had become politicised: many of them had joined the National Union of Mineworkers and had begun to recognise that they

Figure 81. In an attempt to raise awareness of aboriginal heritage, publicity has been given to the idea of returning the remains of Saartje Baartman to the land of her birth. Cape Times *10 April 1995*

HOTTENTOT WOMAN WAS PUT ON DISPLAY

'Return remains' plea

AN ATTEMPT is to be made to bring back to the Cape the remains of a Hottentot woman. **MELANIE GOSLING** reports.

A SOUTH AFRICAN researcher is spearheading a movement to get a Paris museum to return the remains of a Hottentot woman who died in France in 1815 after being on public display for years in Paris and London as a freak.

The skeleton, brains and genitals of Hottentot Saartjie Baartman, who was billed at overseas exhibitions as the Hottentot Venus, are housed in the Musée de l'Homme in Paris.

Pretoria researcher Mr Mansell Upham, who is behind the movement, said yesterday: "Hottentots were seen as the lowest form of human kind, and Saartjie has become a symbol of the dehumanisation of aboriginal peoples.

"We are trying to create a forum to raise awareness about aboriginal heritage in South Africa. Her bones have outlived whatever scientific usefulness they had. We would like to bring her back to the Cape, give her a decent burial and restore her dignity."

Mr Upham, who himself is descended from a Hottentot woman, Eva, niece of Harry the Strandloper, said he had not yet put a request to the museum.

"We should be discussing how to get her back," he said.

Several artists, literary figures and academics had expressed interest in having Saartjie returned to the Cape, he said.

Saartjie Baartman's story is poignant. Not much is known of her origins, but it is believed she came from the Eastern Cape. After being persuaded in 1810 by a ship's surgeon, Alexander Dunlop, to accompany him to England where she was told she could make a fortune by exhibiting herself she died in Paris in 1815 of an "inflammatory and eruptive sickness", having been abandoned to a "showman of wild animals."

Offensive

Historian Percival Kirby found records describing Saartjie being exhibited in London "on a stage two feet high, along which she was led by her keeper, and exhibited like a wild beast, being obliged to walk, stand or sit as he ordered."

Because the exhibition was offensive, the attorney-general called for the Lord Chancellor to intervene, saying Saartjie did not appear to be a free agent.

However, the court found she had come to England freely in exchange for receiving some of the profits of the exhibitions. The decision was based largely on a contract between Saartjie and Dunlop.

Percival believes Saartjie had never

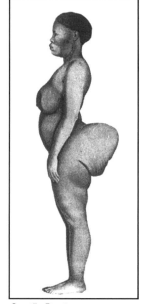

Saartjie Baartman

seen the contract, which he claims Dunlop hastily drew up before the court case.

Saartjie was not only exhibited, but found her way into popular songs and cartoons of the time – mainly because of her huge buttocks. After her death in Paris, at about 28, Frederic Cuvier made a cast of her body, before dissecting it. Saartjie's brain and skeleton were put on display in the Musée de l'Homme, where they remained until they were removed from the public eye.

140

Where are the Khoikhoi today?

There is the well-known story of a tourist visiting Peru who was thrilled to see the remains of the Inca civilization. After travelling extensively throughout the country he eventually took the opportunity while the tour group was waiting at a petrol station to ask the guide 'But where are all the Inca today?' To which the response came: 'Well, one of them is filling up our tank right now.'

This anecdote, which is apparently often told by locals in Peru, pokes fun at the tourist's presumptions and ignorance. His failure to recognise that descendants of the Inca were all around him underlined his presumption that Inca should be racially or culturally 'pure'. It also showed his ignorance of social and historical processes.

We should recognise that the question 'Where are the Khoikhoi today?' rests on similar racist presumptions. Race was not the criterion around which the boundaries of traditional Khoikhoi social and political groups were drawn. The racial and cultural assimilation of outsiders into Khoikhoi society (and vice versa) is therefore entirely expected. There is no reason to suppose that one should find racially or culturally 'pure' Khoikhoi either in the past or the present.

Many people today are proud of their Khoikhoi ancestry and are increasingly seeing it as an important part of their self-identity. To suppose that such identity needs to demonstrate any kind of 'purity' is to be historically uninformed.

Figure 82. Recent efforts to reclaim lost land have received wide publicity. Sunday Times (Cape Metro), 19 March 1995

Queen's help sought in land dispute

BY AYESHA ISMAIL

COLOURED farmers from Namaqualand will hand over a memorandum to the British Consul in Cape Town tomorrow for the attention of the Queen, asking her to use her "influence" to help them have their land returned to them.

The farmers say the land was "unjustly" taken away by the British colonial government in the early 1800s.

The land in question is the subject of a Supreme Court application which will be heard in the Cape Supreme Court tomorrow.

The present owners of the land, De Beers Consolidated Mines Limited, will seek a declaratory order confirming their right to sell the land, which consists of four farms, if they so wish.

The Transitional Local Government – previously the Steinkopf Management Board – will oppose the action.

According to De Beers corporate communications manager Glenn Bryant, the four farms were "acquired"

by De Beers in the 1940s to "secure" their "right" to diamond deposits.

De Beers decided in August 1993 to dispose of the farms due to the limited life of the deposits, he said.

When the land was advertised the management board opposed the sale.

"Despite numerous requests by us for them to substantiate legal right to ownership of the property, they have failed to do so," said Mr Bryant.

"We have now decided to seek legal clarification of this title.

Boeboe van Wyk, spokesman for the Namaqualand Civic Association to which the farmers belong, said they would have nothing to do with the court action as the Supreme Court did not have the jurisdiction to hear land claims.

"We have aboriginal and indigenous title to the land, but this is not recognised by SA law."

Various communities in Namaqualand have an interest in the four farms and other land in the area.

They say they were unjustly dispossessed of their land by the British colonial government in the early 1800s when "they failed to recognise the indigenous peoples right to land."

And despite a regionally organised demand for land, Namaqualanders find themselves outside the immediate parameters of the Department of Land Affairs land reform programmes.

The new Restitution of Land Rights Act does not make provision for land which communities lost before the cut-off date of 1913. The Namaqualanders will also not benefit from the government's Pilot Land Reform Project as it was not in the district chosen for the Northern Cape.

Mr Van Wyk said after a request to meet with the Queen was denied, the farmers decided to hand over a memorandum "asking her to exercise her influence for the return of the land to the indigenous people given that the land was lost through the British colonisation under Queen Victoria."

Figure 83. A future for pastoralism? This photograph of a temporarily vacated stock-station near Pella shows not only the rudiments of the ancient matjieshuis *design, but also the degree of nomadism essential to successful pastoralism in the arid Northern Cape.*

were engaged in a common struggle against mine-owners, rather than competing against other people classified as coloured. And their successful battle against the 'economic units' scheme had boosted their confidence. The struggle over the National Park had a similar effect, not just in the Richtersveld, but on other reserve populations as well.

But the most significant effect seems to have been the realisation that outsiders have begun to acknowledge indigenous land rights. Khoikhoi ancestry, which had for so long been something of a liability, has suddenly become a valuable resource. The international growth of ecotourism, which recognises indigenous populations as an essential part of the environment, has been rapid. The recent boom in tourism in Namaqualand has meant that 'traditional Nama culture', in the form of *matjieshuise*, reed mats and local indigenous knowledge, has the

potential to become a highly marketable asset.

All of these developments have meant that local populations have begun to regain their self-respect and identity. But this does not mean, as some tourists and outsiders are inclined to assume, that they want to return to a 'traditional' lifestyle. The people of the Richtersveld do not see the Park as a sanctuary for the preservation of, or a return to, traditional Khoikhoi culture. Nor is the use of Khoikhoi cultural symbols, such as the *matjieshuis*, indicative of a deep desire to exchange modern dwellings for old. They are not, therefore, saying that they possess a unique Nama (Khoikhoi) culture which sets them apart from others in the region, or elsewhere. Rather, they are acknowledging and professing both their unique history and their common humanity.

Bibliography

Introduction

Elphick, R. H. 1974; 1975. 'The meaning, origin and use of the terms Khoikhoi, San and Khoisan'. *Cabo* 2 (2): 2, 3–7, 12–15.

Raven-Hart, R. 1967. *Before Van Riebeeck: Callers at South Africa from 1488–1652*: 82, 101. Cape Town: Struik.

Chapter 1

Friedman, J. B. 1981. *The Monstrous Races in Medieval Art and Thought*. Cambridge: Harvard University Press.

Humphreys, A. J. B. 1986. *Searching for the Past: The Methods and Techniques of Archaeology*. Cape Town: David Philip.

Raven-Hart, R. 1967. *Before Van Riebeeck*: 42, 19, 20, 100. Cape Town: Struik.

Sealy, J. 1989. 'The use of chemical techniques for reconstructing prehistoric diets: a case study in the south-western Cape'. In: Deacon, J. (ed.) *Goodwin's Legacy*: Goodwin Series 6: 69–76. Cape Town: South African Archaeological Society.

Chapter 2

Cashdan, E. A. 1985. 'Coping with risk: reciprocity among the Basarwa of northern Botswana'. *Man* (new series) 20: 454–474.

Ehret, C. 1982. 'The first spread of food production to southern Africa'. In: Ehret, C. & Posnansky, M. (eds) *The Archaeological and Linguistic Reconstruction of African History*: 158–181. Berkeley: University of California Press.

Elphick, R. 1985. *Khoikhoi and the Founding of White South Africa*. Johannesburg: Ravan.

Hollmann, J. 1993. 'Preliminary report on the Koebee rock paintings, Western Cape Province, South Africa'. *South African Archaeological Bulletin* 48: 16–25.

Kinahan, J. 1991. *Pastoral Nomads of the Central Namib Desert*. Windhoek: New Namibia Books.

Kolb, P. 1731. *The Present State of the Cape of Good Hope*. 2 Vols. London: Innys.

Lee, R. B. 1979. *The !Kung San: Men, Women and Work in a Foraging Society*. Cambridge: Cambridge University Press.

Lichtenstein, H. 1815. *Travels in Southern Africa in the Years 1803, 1804, 1805, 1806*. Cape Town: Van Riebeeck Society, 10 (1928) & 11 (1930).

Mentzel, O. F. 1787. *A Geographical and Topographical Description of the Cape of Good Hope*. Cape Town: Van Riebeeck Society, 25 (1944).

Morris, A. G. 1992. *The Skeletons of Contact: A Study of Protohistoric Burials from the Lower Orange River Valley, South Africa*. Johannesburg: Witwatersrand University Press.

Parkington, J. E. 1984. 'Soaqua and Bushmen: hunters and robbers'. In: Schrire, C. (ed.) *Past and Present in Hunter–Gatherer Studies*: 151–174. New York: Academic Press.

Smith, A. B. 1987. 'Seasonal exploitation of resources on the Vredenburg Peninsula after 2,000 BP'. In: Parkington, J. & M. Hall (eds) *Papers in the Prehistory of the Western Cape, South Africa*: 393–402. Oxford: British Archaeological Reports, International Series 332.

Smith, A. B. 1993. 'Exploitation of marine mammals by prehistoric Cape herders'. *South African Journal of Science* 89: 162–165.

Stow, G. W. 1905. *The Native Races of South Africa: A History of the Intrusion of the Hottentots and Bantu into the Hunting Grounds of the Bushmen, the Aborigines of the Country*. London: Swan Sonnenschein.

Wilmsen, E. N. 1989. *Land Filled with Flies: A Political Economy of the Kalahari*: 65. Chicago: Chicago University Press.

Chapter 3

Katz, R. 1982. *Boiling Energy: Community Healing among the Kalahari !Kung*: 251–252. Cambridge, Mass.: Harvard University Press.

Smith, A. B. 1990. 'On becoming herders: Khoikhoi and San ethnicity in southern Africa'. *African Studies*, (Wits) 49, 2: 51–73.

Thom, H. B. 1952. *The Journal of Jan van Riebeeck*, I: 176. 3 Vols, Cape Town: Balkema.

Chapter 4

Barnard, A. 1992. *Hunters and Herders of Southern Africa: A Comparative Ethnography of the Khoisan Peoples*. Cambridge: Cambridge University Press.

Beaman, A. W. 1983. 'Women's participation in pastoral economy: income maximisation among the Rendille'. *Nomadic Peoples* 12: 20–25.

Carstens, P., G. Klinghardt and M. West (eds). *Trails in the Thirstland: The Anthropological Field Diaries of Winifred Hoernlé*. Cape Town, Centre for African Studies, University of Cape Town.

Engelbrecht, J. A. 1936. *The Korana: An Account of their Customs and their History, with Texts*. Cape Town: Maskew Miller.

Hoernlé, A. W. 1913. *Richtersveld, the Land and its People*. Johannesburg: Council of Education, Witwatersrand.

Schapera, I. 1930. *The Khoisan Peoples of South Africa: Bushmen and Hottentots*. London: George Routledge & Sons.

Smith, A. B. and R. H. Pheiffer. 1992. 'Col. Robert Gordon's notes on the Khoikhoi, 1779–80'. *Annals of the South African Cultural History Museum* 5, 1.

Stow, G. W. 1905. *The Native Races of South Africa: A History of the Intrusion of the Hottentots and Bantu into the Hunting Grounds of the Bushmen, the Aborigines of the Country*. London: Swan Sonnenschein.

Wilson, M. and L. Thompson (eds) 1969. *The Oxford History of South Africa*. Oxford: Clarendon Press.

Chapter 5

Elphick, R. 1985. *Khoikhoi and the Founding of White South Africa*. Johannesburg: Ravan Press.

Lupton, J. H. (ed.) 1895. *The Utopia of Sir Thomas More*: 154–155. Oxford: Clarendon Press.

Moodie, D. (ed.) 1960. *The Record ... Condition and Treatment of the Native Tribes of South Africa*, I: 4, 5, 7, 8. 2 Vols. Cape Town: Balkema.

New Dictionary of South African Biography for Coree.

Raven-Hart, R. 1967. *Before Van Riebeeck: Callers at South Africa from 1488 to 1652*: 1–10, 13–14, 23, 30, 32, 40, 47, 64, 67, 70–71, 74–75, 76–77, 78, 82, 83, 84, 88, 124, 175, 177, 178. Cape Town: Struik.

Chapter 6

Bredekamp, H. C. 1982. *Van Veeverskappers tot Veewagters, 'n Historiese ondersoek na Betrekkinge tussen die Khoikhoi en Europeers aan die Kaap, 1662–1679*. Bellville: Die Wes Kaaplandse Instituut vir Historiese Navorsing.

Elphick, R. & H. Giliomee (eds) 1989. *The Shaping of South African Society, 1652–1840*. Cape Town: Maskew Miller Longman.

Elphick, R. 1985. *Khoikhoi and the Founding of White South Africa*. Johannesburg: Ravan Press.

Malherbe, V. C. 1990. *Krotoa, Called 'Eva': A Woman Between*, Cape Town: University of Cape Town, Centre for African Studies, Communications No. 19/1990.

Moodie, D. (ed.) 1960. *The Record ... Condition and Treatment of the Native Tribes of South Africa*: I: 10, 11, 13, 272. 2 Vols. Cape Town: Balkema.

New Dictionary of South African Biography for Harry/Autshumato, Doman, Eva/Krotoa, Gonnema, Oedasoa, Gogosoa, Klaas/Dorha.

Raven-Hart, R. 1971. *Cape Good Hope, 1652–1702, The First Fifty Years of Dutch Colonisation as seen by Callers*. Cape Town: Balkema.

Shell, R. C. H. 1994. *Children of Bondage*: 362. Johannesburg: Witwatersrand University Press.

Thom, H. B. (ed.) 1952. *Journal of Jan van Riebeeck*. 3 Vols. Cape Town: Balkema.

There are now many works analysing the pictorial and written representation of the Khoikhoi and the San, for example:

Coetzee, J. M. 1988. *White Writing: On the Culture of Letters in South Africa*: ch. 1. Radix/ Yale University Press.

Smith, A. B. 1983. 'The Hotnot syndrome: myth-making in South African school textbooks'. *Social Dynamics*: 9, 2: 37–49.

Van Wyk Smith, M. 1992. '"The most wretched of the human race": the iconography of the Khoikhoin (Hottentots) 1500–1800'. *History and Anthropology* 5: 285–330.

Chapter 7

Abrahams, Y. 1994. 'Resistance, pacification and consciousness: a discussion of the historiography of Khoisan resistance from 1972 to 1993 and Khoisan resistance from 1652 to 1853': 38–9, 41. MA thesis, Queen's University, Ontario, Canada.

Bredekamp, H. C. 1987. 'Vehettge Tikkuie, alias Moeder Lena van Genadendal, 1739–1800'. *Quarterly Bulletin of the South African Library* 41, 4: 134–141.

Harinck, G. 1969. 'Interaction between Xhosa and Khoi: emphasis on the period 1620–1750'. In Thompson L. (ed.) *African Societies in Southern Africa*. London: Heinemann.

Marais, J. S. 1939, 1968. *The Cape Coloured People, 1652–1937*. Johannesburg: Witwatersrand University Press.

Moodie, *The Record*: (3): 3; (5): 10.

New Dictionary of South African Biography for Africo Christian, Adam Kok I, II and III, Cornelis Kok I and II.

Newton-King, S. 1992. 'The enemy within: the struggle for ascendancy on the Cape Eastern Frontier, 1760–1799'. PhD thesis, School of Oriental and African Studies, University of London.

Penn, N. 1989. 'Labour, land and livestock in the Western Cape during the eighteenth century: the Khoisan and the colonists'. In James, W. G. & Simons M. (eds) *The Angry Divide: Social and Economic History of the Western Cape*. Cape Town: David Philip.

Chapter 8

Adhikari, M. 1992. 'The sons of Ham: slavery and the making of coloured identity'. *South African Historical Journal* 27: 95–112.

Adhikari, M. 1992. 'God, Jan van Riebeeck and "the Coloured People": the anatomy of a South African joke'. *Southern African Discourse* 4, 3: 4–10.

Anderson, B. 1985. *Imagined Communities, Reflections on the Origin and Spread of Nationalism*: 14. London: Verso.

Boyce, W. B. 1838, 1971. *Notes on South African Affairs, from 1834 to 1838*: 127. Grahamstown: Aldum & Harvey, reprinted Cape Town: Struik.

Crais, C. C. 1992. *The Making of the Colonial Order: White Supremacy and Black Resistance in the Eastern Cape, 1770–1865*. Johannesburg: Witwatersrand University Press.

Crais, C. C. 1994. 'Slavery and emancipation in the Eastern Cape'. In Worden, N. & Crais, C. (eds) *Breaking the Chains: Slavery and its Legacy in the Nineteenth–Century Cape Colony*: pp.??? Johannesburg: Witwatersrand University Press.

Duly, L. C. 1972. 'A revisit with the Cape's Hottentot Ordinance of 1828'. In Kooy M. (ed.) *Studies in Economics and Economic History*. London: Macmillan.

Du Toit, A. & H. Giliomee (eds). 1983. *Afrikaner Political Thought, Analysis and Documents, I, 1780–1850*: 111. Cape Town: David Philip.

Elbourne, E. 1992. 'Early Khoisan uses of mission Christianity'. *Kronos* 19: 3–27.

Elbourne, E. 1994. 'Freedom at issue: vagrancy legislation and the meaning of freedom in Britain and the Cape Colony, 1799–1842'. *Slavery and Abolition, A Journal of Slave and Post-Slave Studies* 15, 2: 114–150.

Kirby R. 1949, 1954. 'The Hottentot Venus'. *Africana Notes and News* 6, 3 and 11, 5.

Kirk, A. 1985. 'The Cape economy and the expropriation of the Kat River Settlement, 1846–53'. In Marks, S. and Atmore, A. (eds) *Economy and Society in pre-industrial South Africa*. London: Longman.

New Dictionary of South African Biography for Boezak, Klaas Stuurman, David Stuurman, Britanje Jantjes, Cupido Kakkerlak, Andries Stoffels, Andries Botha, Andries Abraham Stockenstrom le Fleur.

Newton-King, S. and Malherbe, V. C. 1981. *The Khoikhoi Rebellion in the Eastern Cape (1799–1803)*. Cape Town: University of Cape Town, Centre for African Studies.

Newton-King, S. 1985. 'The labour market of the Cape Colony, 1807–28'. In Marks, S. and Atmore, A. (eds) *Economy and Society in Pre–industrial South Africa*. London: Longman.

Nasson, B. 1991. *Abraham Esau's War: A Black South African's war in the Cape, 1899–1902*. Cape Town: David Philip.

Sales, J. 1975. *Mission Stations and the Coloured Communities of the Eastern Cape, 1800–1852*. Cape Town: Balkema.

Shaw, B. 1970. *Memorials of South Africa*: 60, 281–20. Cape Town: Struik.

Strauss, T. 1979. *War along the Orange*. Cape Town: Centre for African Studies Communications 1, University of Cape Town.

Trapido, S. 1964. 'The origins of the Cape franchise qualifications of 1853'. *Journal of African History*: 37–54.

Trapido, S. 1992. 'The emergence of liberalism and the making of "Hottentot nationalism", 1815–1834.', *Collected Seminar Papers* 42. Institute of Commonwealth Studies: University of London.

Wannenburgh, A. *Forgotten Frontiersmen*. Cape Town: Howard Timmins.

The study of Saartjie Baartman is a growth industry. For example, see:

Lindfors, B. 1985. 'Courting the Hottentot Venus', *Africa* 40: 133–148.

Sander, L. G. 1986. 'Black bodies, white bodies: toward an iconography of female sexuality in late nineteenth-century art, medicine, and literature'. In Gates H. L. Jr. (ed.) *'Race', Writing, and Difference*. Chicago: University of Chicago Press.

Chapter 9

Carstens, W. P. 1966. *The Social Structure of a Cape Coloured Reserve*. Cape Town: Oxford University Press.

Japha, D., Japha, V., Le Grange, L., Todeschini, F. 1993. *Mission Settlements in South Africa*.

Smalberger, J. M. 1975. *A History of Copper Mining in Namaqualand, 1846–1931*. Struik, Cape Town.

Strassberger, E. 1969. *The Rhenish Mission Society in South Africa, 1830–1950*. Struik, Cape Town.

Van der Horst, S. (ed.) 1976. *The Theron Commission Report (Summary of Commission of Enquiry into matters relating to the Coloured Population Group)*. Johannesburg: S. A. Institute of Race Relations.

Van der Waal-Braaksma, G. and Ferreira, O.J.O. 1986. *Die Noordweste: Die Stoftelike Kultuuruitinge van die Streek se Bewoners*. Johannesburg: Genootskap vir Afrikaanse Volkskunde.

Chapter 10

Carstens, W. P. 1966. *The Social Structure of a Cape Coloured Reserve*. Cape Town: Oxford University Press.

Krone, H. and Steyn, L. 1991. *Land Use in Namaqualand*. Athlone: Surplus People Project.

Marais, J. S. 1968. *The Cape Coloured People: 1652–1937*. Johannesburg: Witwatersrand University Press.

Smith, A. B. (ed.) 1995. *Einiqualand: Studies of the Orange River Frontier*. Cape Town: University of Cape Town Press.

Klinghardt, G. P. 1994. 'Death in Pella, mortuary rituals in a Namaqualand reserve, 1978–1989'. *Annals of the South African History Museum*: 104, 6.

Index